WENDY

MW00881600

Nann
5-2018

thin places – celtic

LOVE AFTER DEATH

Healing Grief
Through Afterlife Communication

Wheat

A symbol of life everlasting...

ISBN-10: 1466383348
EAN-13: 9781466383340

CONTENTS

ACKNOWLEDGEMENTS

First and foremost, I wish to thank my mum and dad, Barbara and Kenneth Marshall, who always taught me to think of reasons why I 'should'. I love you both dearly, always.

My heartfelt thanks also go to the many wonderful people who have reached inside themselves to find the courage and the words to tell their stories for this book. You are truly amazing. Your stories have touched me in a very special way. Many of you I have never met, yet you have trusted me with your deepest most personal experiences. Thank you.

I also need to thank Lyn Macintosh for giving me the 'push' to start. Your keen enthusiasm never faltered. Your diligent editing of my 'creative' spelling has brought this book up to scratch. I could not have done it without you!

Giacomo Pesaturo, who patiently listened whilst I outlined the gist of my book and came up with *The Boy With No Shadow*. What can I say? Grazie mille!

To my sister, Pauline, who spells just as creatively as I do, but whose brilliant eye for structure helped shape this book.

And of course, to those who share my life most closely, my husband, David, and our darling daughter, Jessica. You have helped in more ways than I can say. You are both always in my heart.

THE BOY WITH NO SHADOW

By Giacomo Pesaturo

JOURNEY

The boy's name was not important. There was nobody there to call his name anyway. He lived in a small hut made of wood; mud and tree branches covered the round hole that served as a roof. Still rain got in at times, but the boy did not mind. He was proud of his hut.

When you have been cast away from your village and your own people refuse to even acknowledge you, it is important to have something to be proud of. And he was proud of his hut; he had built it all by himself. And he was proud that he was a good hunter. He was not afraid to enter the wood and procure his own food. He had even learned to discern between edible plants and poisonous ones.

It is not easy to learn without an elder to show and teach you. But there was nothing he could do about that. In his heart he knew it was not his fault that he did not have a Shadow, but the tribe thought differently.

Since the beginning of time, the tribe had dictated that a boy who lost his parents before reaching maturity was described as 'without a Shadow'. It was believed that there was nothing left to keep him grounded, to keep him connected to the tribe and the village duties. His link to the group was broken; it was believed that his soul would wander endlessly, not knowing where to go.

It was said by the elders that at night, when only the wind blowing through the trees of the surrounding forest could be heard, spirits visited the village to seek people without a Shadow.

The boy was sad. When at the age of ten his parents were killed by an old tree that fell on the family hut, crushing them, his life had changed forever. Still he carried the guilt. Playing with friends near the river with the other kids, there was nothing he could have done to save his parents. He felt he should have been able to have done something.

Shame was also present in his heart. Now he was different from the other boys.

He still remembered the day after the bodies of his parents were cremated just outside the village. He remembered the sad looks a few of the old women gave him. He remembered the words of the village chief as he was led away from the tribe: 'Boy, from today you have no Shadow. From today you do not belong here anymore. You are not allowed back in the village – your wandering soul will bring us bad luck. Go now, and may your Shadow find you.'

As he sat there, alone outside his hut, listening to the guttural sounds of monkeys in the forest, he felt lonely. It felt like time was holding a sharp chisel, carving a bit more of his soul every day, leaving a hole that could never be filled again.

What is the purpose of this? The boy sat and thought for a while. *What is the reason for me to get up and face each long and lonely day? How can I go on? Will I ever find my Shadow again?*

Looking at the empty space surrounding him, something stirred inside. A deep river of loss filled his soul and he felt a sense of hopelessness he had never experienced before.

Journey

Only one thought kept returning, over and over. *What is the point?* Like a mantra, it swirled around his mind as he collected water, as he picked berries to eat, as he made a fire to keep large animals away at night.

What is the point? He asked himself as he fell asleep.

The next morning the boy felt different. A *different* thought was now in his mind. *If there is no point, and my soul is meant to wander aimlessly, I may as well start wandering now!*

And that was that. He placed some branches over the entrance of his hut to prevent wild animals from claiming it as their home. He took his possessions, a hunting knife made of wood with a sharp rock as a blade, the wolf skin that kept him warm at night, and a wooden bowl he had carved for himself to collect water. That was it. He was ready to go.

Maybe, he thought, *if I go I will leave my loneliness behind.*

Casting a last look at the place that had been his home for the last five years, he went forward, cutting through the tall grass. Towards the wood, towards the shade of the trees, towards a day with no tomorrow.

IN THE BEGINNING

For death begins with life's first breath
And life begins at touch of death...

John Oxenham

IN THE BEGINNING

Softly, long before you kiss me
Long before your arms can beg me stay
For one more hour or one more day.
After all the years, I can't bear the tears
To fall, so softly as I leave you there...

Softly

Hal Shaper and Antonio DeVita and Giorgio Calabrese

"I got up during the night to go to the toilet,' said my father in his broad Yorkshire accent, 'and our Donald and our Arthur were standing there.'

We are standing in the lounge room, my father and I, and he points to where his brothers had stood the night before. 'I wasn't scared, not frightened. I sat down in the middle of the lounge. I thought they'd sit either side of me, but they didn't. They didn't speak and they didn't move. They just looked at me.'

My dad goes on, 'So I started talking to them, in my head, because I knew they couldn't really be there.' And so he should know. My uncle Donald had been dead for close to thirty years, my uncle Arthur, not quite ten. No, they definitely couldn't really be there, could they?

'But they looked so real. They were solid, like you are. I couldn't see through them like the ghosts you see on the telly. They were as real as you are,' he stated emphatically. My dad did not believe in ghosts. He was vaguely interested in other people's experiences, but they always happened to other people, not to him. This was different. This was him.

And somewhere in the back of his mind he knew why they might be there. 'I'm not bloody going with *you!*' he told them, and went back to bed leaving his two brothers, Donald and Arthur, still standing in his lounge room. Watching.

This experience is part of the phenomena called nearing-death awareness. It naturally occurs when a person is moving towards death and may include seeing and communicating with loved ones who have already died, or other spiritual beings, and the use of symbolic language to describe the impending journey.

Only a couple of months later my dad was to come to me again with a similar experience. I visited my parents often and on this particular occasion he had written down what he'd experienced the previous night. After going to the toilet in the middle of the night he had encountered his brothers once more. This time it was different. They had spoken to him. They had given him part of a number, but wouldn't give him the rest. He was distressed that he couldn't have the rest of the number – he desperately wanted the whole number, and begged to have it.

With tears streaming down his face he asked me what I thought this meant. I remember thinking, *Oh God, I don't know what to say.* My immediate thought was, *your number's up, you're going to die*, but I couldn't say that.

I thought for a moment about the symbolism of only a partial number being given, and I said, 'I think it means your number's not up yet; that's why they only gave you part of the number.' Neither of us had any inkling as to how relevant this event would be.

Two or three days later Dad haemorrhaged from a burst ulcer in his stomach. As he was taking Warfarin (an anticoagulant) he lost a lot of blood and was told by doctors that he had nearly died. I visited him in hospital and he was sitting up in bed saying to me with a big smile, 'You were right, my number's not up.' He was ecstatic. Not only was his time not quite up, but he had experienced something that was special, that could not help but change the way in which he perceived his impending journey.

On the January 9th, 2008, his brothers finally had their way, paying one last visit, and while napping on the lounge, TV on, he slipped away with them so peacefully that it was several hours before Mum even noticed he'd gone.

What a way to go! My dad was scared of dying and, like most of us, just didn't want to go. The tears would roll down his face as we were leaving after one of our visits – thinking he may not see us again, that he would die before we made the next trip. He was grieving his own leaving of us. Grieving his own loss of life. And he was very scared. I think it is poetic that in the end he left so...softly.

During my bereavement I was to ponder what had taken place leading up to my dad's death. Questions niggled at my mind. Were these events somehow produced by a combination of drugs, poor health and old age, merely a trick of the mind? Or were the ghostly visits the reality, and death the illusion?

These experiences had subtly softened the blow for me somehow; I drew strength from them, and just to add more to the mixing pot that was brewing within my mind, during the months of grief that followed I was to receive several 'visits' of my own from my father. I will relate these in detail a little later in the book. These however, unlike his brotherly visitations, did not surprise me in the least. I invited him, in my mind. Because I knew if his brothers could visit, then so could he, and my dad, never one to disappoint, responded – spectacularly!

For me, writing this book is a journey into myself. If anyone had ever told me 10 years ago, or even two or three years ago for that matter, that I would write a book about death I would have dismissed it in an instant. You see, death has been my greatest fear since being very small. My imagination has run riot all my life. Only more recently have I finally laid to rest my fears and fantasies, by facing the very thing that has terrorised me.

That said, in hindsight 'something' has been trying to get my attention for a very long time; this book has been brewing beneath the surface for many years. I think in some way I have always known that this moment would come. So here I find myself, writing about the thing that has haunted me for most of my life. I think it is significant that even my career choice, being a hypnotherapist and counsellor, has given me a deeper understanding of grief and bereavement and has nicely propelled me to where I stand today.

This book, *Love after Death*, is about actively engaging in a positive relationship with someone who has died. Some people just do it naturally (we call them mediums) but this is not to say that this capacity to commune with someone who has died is only available to the select and gifted few. We can all do it. We can all draw back the perceived thin veil that separates the living from the dead. For our loved ones who have died, contact with us is a normal, natural occurrence. It's a given, nothing 'supernatural' or 'paranormal' here. Sometimes we, the living, have more difficulty with this concept.

It is my intention to write a book that will examine death from many different perspectives and facets, offering new ways of perceiving the relationship you have with loved ones who have died. It is my hope that this book will give you permission to never let go, inspire and give you the courage to find ways of staying connected: talking, listening and laughing with your loved one. A relationship does not cease to exist because of death. Love does not cease to exist because of death. Love is eternal and never dies. Many of the extraordinary stories told by people in this book are testament to this.

This book is also about finding the peace within yourself to *accept* — accept that you haven't *lost* anything, **only that your relationship**

has now changed. It is about allowing, indeed nurturing, this new relationship, enabling it to flourish and grow and ultimately for it to be fully embraced into your life. It is about reaching out and meeting your loved ones halfway in *their* endeavours to contact you.

This book is for you if a loved one has died. It does not matter whether this was ten days, ten weeks or ten years ago. This book is for you if you would like to learn how to keep the lines of communication open with your loved one, even though they have died. This book is for you if you have ever felt that you have communicated with someone who has died, have had a near-death experience or indeed are just curious about the phenomena and extraordinary experiences that normal people have when faced with grieving or with dying. This book is also for you if you are supporting someone who is grieving or someone who is dying.

Death, like life, is a spiritual experience, one that each and every one of us will face at some time on our own journey. Without a spiritual belief, death and the 'nothingness' that we may perceive it to be, can be downright terrifying. It is therefore in our best interests to have a spiritual belief, to know intimately what this belief is, to be able to trust it to serve us when we need it most. Our beliefs are important, they shape how we deal with life, how we 'cope' through the dark and difficult times. This is never so true as when faced with the death of a loved one. I hope, then, that this work will help you to be able to define your beliefs, what works for you, and help you to 'know' yourself better because of this understanding.

This book, *Love after Death,* is in four parts. I encourage you to read each in sequential order, as each part follows on from the previous one. This book is a journey. Like a single drop of rain at the top of a mountain, following each curve and crevice on its way to the mighty ocean, allow yourself the luxury of taking the time to meander over each chapter. Enjoy and savour the experience of each part.

The natural place, then, to commence our journey, is at the top of the mountain. Starting with the raindrops that are our tears, Part 1, *The Illusion*, explores the intricate nature of grief and bereavement and the spiritual experience that has been called death, and offers simple steps to help navigate us through these difficult times. I have called it *The Illusion* because it is so easy to be caught up in the machinations of our bereavement that we simply do not see anything outside our own predicament. We think and feel that we are somehow left alone, isolated and lost. As we will explore in the remainder of the book, this is simply not true.

Part 2, *The Reality*, is about opening the window of our perceptions and listening with our hearts to the very *real* stories of those who have experienced nearing-death awareness, near-death experiences and after-death communication. These stories give us hope and offer a special glimpse through the doorway of our grief at the amazing phenomena surrounding death and bereavement.

In Part 3, entitled *The Science*, we are introduced to the concepts of quantum physics, how it relates to our understanding of the phenomena surrounding death and explore some of the latest groundbreaking research into nearing-death awareness, near-death experiences and after-death communication. We take a fascinating look at what is actually happening within our brain at the moment of death as we cross that threshold into the realm of spirit.

What begins with a tiny raindrop in Part 1 now thrusts us deeper into the mystery of the great ocean that is spirit. Part 4, *The Rainbow,* offers step-by-step ways of tapping into the infinite realms of the subconscious mind in order to connect with your loved one who has died.

Whilst writing this book I have been fortunate to be contacted by many people who have kindly donated their own fascinating stories to this work. Many of the occurrences that are outlined take place during grief or when a person is close to death. For most of us these are highly stressful events, the most stressful a human may ever encounter during their earthly life. In the very depths of despair I do not believe that anyone makes up stories about their loved ones, so as you, like me, raise an eyebrow and think that perhaps they are 'over the top', ask yourself this: *when, in your life, have you made a story up when you are in the depths of despair?* In times of crisis you are fighting for your sanity and just, only just, making it through each day. Surviving – barely. Certainly not in the mood for imaginings or creating tales. It is with this in mind that I ask you to accept each and every one of these stories on its own merits.

I have sought, wherever possible, to include stories in their entirety. I have encouraged contributors to write in their own style, telling their own stories in their own words. Occasionally stories have been 'trimmed' to ensure the book does in fact come to an end.

Throughout this book you will notice simple meditations, activities or reflections. Each one is a gift to you. I urge you now to do them as you journey through the book. They are specifically designed to facilitate self-healing, self-nurturing and spiritual awareness and to move you towards connecting with your loved one in a very special way. They are also specifically designed to be simple. If you purchase a small journal or some other writing material you can record your experiences for reflection. So make a commitment, set aside the time and complete each one. You are worth it. And so is your loved one!

Woven throughout the book is the tale of a small boy with a big heart. When we are bereaved, we too, like the boy in this story, may feel as if we have lost a part of ourselves, our shadow, that we are somehow no longer whole or complete. *The Boy With No Shadow* gently reminds us that what we seek is within, that we are never truly alone and that all we need do is simply give ourselves the permission, the space and the courage to open our hearts and our minds to what is. It is my sincerest wish for you that, as you journey through this book, you too, like the boy, discover that which you seek.

Enjoy the trip!

Part 1

THE ILLUSION

Reality is merely an illusion, although a very persistent one...

Albert Einstein

Lost

The boy walked for almost two days through the thick forest, resting every few hours whenever he found some running water. The only company he had was the sound coming from deep inside the tree branches. He was used to this, having spent many hours alone, waiting for any stray animal that he could hunt for food.

Walking briskly the boy noticed the trees becoming sparser with more light coming in from above, less noise from the birds. Eventually, leaving the forest behind him, he arrived at a clearing. As he stepped out onto the soft grass, momentarily blinded by the daylight, he looked around. In front of him the countryside stretched ahead, gentle hills at his left and right, a gentle slope in the centre with a well worn path in its middle.

The boy had never been here before. He was not sure in which direction to go. A part of him wanted to follow the path, see where it went. The other part of him thought that it was probably best to head for the hills, so as not to encounter anybody. He did not know if someone inhabited this area, but he was conscious that he did not have a Shadow, regardless of where he was.

But he knew that his curiosity would win. He had been alone for so long that even a dangerous encounter was better than solitude. He slowly started walking along the edge of the path, anticipation quickly growing in his mind.

Almost at the end of the day, when dusk started to settle in, the boy arrived at a bend in the path. Around the bend, off in the distance, he saw a long stone wall. Even from here the boy could tell it was high, at least the height of two fully grown men. He knew also that he was afraid, but he had come too far to turn back now. He decided to make camp for the night, without lighting a fire, lest he be seen from far away. He would decide the best course of action in the morning.

The first morning light found the boy already awake. He had slept little, afraid of wild animals and strange people that may be passing by. He started on the path again, moving in the direction of the wall. *What will I find there? Will I be captured and kept as a slave? Will I be killed?* Many questions filtered through his mind.

As he moved closer to the large wall he noticed that there was an opening in it, just large enough to let pass a man and an ox, together side by side. Near the entrance, sitting on the ground, he saw a figure. Probably a keeper or a sentinel of some tribe, he thought. His feet wanted to stop, his mind confused, but his resolve stood firm. He kept walking.

When he finally arrived near the opening he could see that the figure sitting in the shadow of the wall was an old woman. He felt better. *Surely I am stronger than an old woman,* he thought. His shoulders relaxed a bit and his heart stopped fluttering.

He stood near the woman. She quickly looked up at him, smiled and just as quickly looked away. Even though her glance had been so rapid, the boy saw that her eyes were moist, as if she had just finished crying. The boy did not know what to do, or say. Whenever he was feeling sad he did not want anybody to know. But he was a man, she was a woman, and in his village the women cried openly when tragedy struck. Man did not. This was a sign of weakness.

Because he did not know what to do, the boy sat on the ground near, but not too close, to the woman. He hoped she would say something first. And she did.

'What have you lost, boy?' she said and looked him straight in the eyes, a certainty in her voice, like she already knew the answer.

'What makes you think I lost something, old lady?' The boy replied, trying to sound sure of himself.

'All the people that go wandering past the forest and find themselves here have lost something. And they hope that they may find it here.' She held her gaze on him. 'What is it that you believe you have lost? Your courage? Your honour? Your love?'

The boy knew that telling her his story may mean that he would be sent away from here too. And what if she did not believe that it wasn't his fault that he had lost his Shadow? But something in her demeanour, compounded with all the time he had been alone, made him trust her. He told his story in whispers, even though no-one else was around to hear.

When he had finished, his own eyes were also moist, but he was determined not to cry in front of a woman.

The old woman let some time pass in silence, and after a while she took the boy's hand in her own. *Old hands, wrinkled hands*, the boy thought, *but they remind me of my own grandmother*, and he felt warm.

The old woman's voice was soft as she started to speak, almost hypnotic, and the boy was soon wrapped in a cadence of soft velvet. The boy listened.

'You are robbed of your Shadow only by the pain you feel in your heart. The depth of your pain is the measure of your loss. It means that you have loved and this is indeed a gift beyond price. It will take great courage to seek out and find that which you think you have lost.'

Although he did not really understand the old lady, the boy was intrigued. She spoke of hope, hope that he could find his shadow.

The boy thought for a moment. 'So where should I go, what should I do? I will do anything to find my shadow so one day I may return to the village I love.' The boy felt awkward asking as he did not want to appear stupid.

But the woman answered with a question, 'Why is it that you look outside for that which can only be found within?'

The boy's confusion soared. Seeing this, the old woman got up, picked up a tree branch that was lying nearby and walked up to the opening in the wall. In the dry mud she started scratching with the piece of wood, repeatedly, until a deep groove was formed. She stopped, and looking at him said, 'Cross the furrow to the other side when it is dark. It is easy to cross when the sun shines, but when it is dark and cold, crossing is harder.'

Leaning on the tree branch she was still holding, she spoke softly, 'Wait here until night falls. You will see a light coming through the entrance. Listen to your heart at that moment. It will either tell you to cross, or to walk away. You will know what to do. Trust the voice that talks to you when you are alone.' She slowly started to move away from him. 'And if you decide to cross, you will hear more voices, voices you will believe. And you will understand.'

She whispered a few words that the boy did not understand and, without another word, walked away following the edge of the wall.

The boy stood, confused for a moment, then sat where the old woman had been, and waited. Waited for the darkness to come, and for the light to shine.

one

BUTTERFLIES

Death is not extinguishing the light;
it is putting out the lamp because the dawn has come.

Rabindranath Tagore

Dying is the most natural thing in the world to do. We all do it.
Everyone. No exceptions. Yet our whole society is geared up to
postpone this normal, natural occurrence from happening, to prolong
life at all cost to dignity and quality of life. We fight to the bitter
end.

Bereavement is for those who are left behind. Like the little boy in
the Pied Piper, we are left to stand alone and sobbing before the great
mountain. Paradise denied. The door is closed. We are crippled, not
by our lameness but by our sorrow.

And for others – What to say? How to help? What to do? And
in the 'saying' and the 'helping' and the 'doing' we too are forced to
look at our own mortality. And we don't like this. It's uncomfortable.

Fear prevails. The desire to run like hell is overwhelming. And the more we try to get away from death and all that it encompasses, the more fear we feel. The truth is there ain't no way to get away from death and its intimate companions, grief and bereavement. The other truth is that fear loves the company of ignorance. So the question then becomes not *how do we get away?* but, *how do we be still? How do we shine the light on our deepest, darkest fears? How do we find our peace?*

So with open heart and mind, we begin with the first step on our journey. And there really is only one place to start, and so it is that we begin with a very special person, a pioneer in the area of bereavement, grief and dying – Elizabeth Kübler-Ross.

At the very tender age of 19, Elizabeth Kübler-Ross, a self-professed young and ignorant youth, visited a concentration camp in Maidanek, Poland. What she saw carved or drawn in chalk or rock on the walls of the concentration camp, by children facing death, were butterflies. In her own words she tells us, 'I saw those butterflies. I was young. I was very ignorant. I had no idea why five, six, seven, eight, nine-year-old children who were taken away from home, from their parents, from the security of their homes and schools into cattle cars, and shipped to Auschwitz and Buchenwald and Maidanek, why these children should see butterflies. It took me a quarter of a century to find the answer. Maidanek was the beginning of my work.'

Elisabeth Kübler-Ross was to go on to become a psychiatrist and the world's first expert in death, dying and bereavement, working tirelessly throughout her life with dying children, adults and their bereaved families. The experience at Maidanek profoundly affected Elisabeth Kübler-Ross and was her first taste of the unique and special symbolic language used by the dying. The cocoon, she discovered, symbolically represents the physical body, which temporarily houses the soul. When we die, the butterfly or soul, which is beautiful, emerges and flies free.

It was to be a fellow named Dr Raymond Moody, a psychologist and medical doctor, who, after conducting extensive research with people who had clinically died and were subsequently brought back from the brink of death, was the first to bring to the attention of the world the concept of near-death experiences, in his book *Life after Life*. Upon reading his work, Elisabeth Kübler-Ross noted that the findings and conclusions he had come to regarding life after death matched her own findings through working with the dying and the bereaved. This was to begin a search, by Elisabeth Kübler-Ross, into the nature of life and death and resulted in an ongoing study throughout the remainder of her lifelong work.

It was Elisabeth Kübler-Ross who first introduced the concept of what she called the Five Stages of Grief: denial, anger, bargaining, depression and acceptance, in her groundbreaking book, *On Death and Dying*, in 1969. Until this time, we were largely in the Dark Ages when it came to grief and bereavement – not much had been written about the subject. It is 40 years since this seminal work, and it is still as relevant today as ever. Sadly though, The Five Stages of Grief have been misunderstood for much of this time.

The Five Stages of Grief represents a model of how people grieve; it helps to give foundation to our understanding of the grieving process. It is the very nature of such a representation that has created such controversy. It implies that in our grief we will move in a sequential order through each phase, passing through one and then another until we have completed each. This could not be further from the truth. The exquisite nature of grief ensures that there is no set format, no rules, no correct or incorrect way to be in grief – it simply takes its course, and is unconcerned with any form we may try to impose on it.

The truth is that there is no 'correct' way to 'do' grief. Grief is as individual and unique as a fingerprint and no two people will experience it in quite the same manner. Grief is complex and illogical, a messy business that can wreak havoc in our lives at a moment's notice. There is never time to prepare, and all the knowledge and learning does little to prime us for the convoluted and intricate experience we call grief.

I remember, in the year preceding my father's death, how I would think to myself *Wendy, Dad is probably going to die soon. I'll be OK because forewarned is forearmed. I know it's going to happen, so it won't be such a shock.* Yet at 10.30 one evening, when I was awoken by the dreaded phone call, I was in shock. I was not prepared.

Nor can we possibly imagine what it will be like when someone we love deeply is no longer with us physically. It is unimaginable, incomprehensible, and our lives are never quite the same again.

But the Kübler-Ross model *is* useful, in that it gives insight into what are very normal reactions, what we may experience as part of the grieving process. It gives a framework, tools to understand some of what we might be experiencing. It allows us to be able to say to ourselves, *What I am feeling is part of grief. I'm not losing my marbles, not going crazy,* and to begin to understand that it's okay for us to feel whatever it is we feel. It gives us permission to say, *I'm not a freak, this is not unusual, it's quite normal to feel this way. I'm not going mad.* It allows us to identify what we may be feeling and say *Ah, this is a normal part of grief,* when our world has been kicked upside down and we feel like we are losing our grip on sanity.

The Five Stages of Grief was never intended to categorise people, or to tell people what they should, or shouldn't, be feeling. Neither was it intended to be followed in any sequential manner. We may experience only one or two of the stages, or we may experience all of them or none of them. The stages may weave in and out of our lives for many years or for just a short time. Grief has no agenda.

So now let's take a brief look at the Five Stages of Grief: denial, anger, bargaining, depression and acceptance.

DENIAL

Originally the concept of denial referred to the person who was in the process of dying, and certainly this is one of the stages that we may go through as we approach death. Coming to terms with our own prospects regarding death is certainly daunting and many of us would prefer to skip death altogether! But this stage is also very relevant for the person who is in grief as they deny the loss of the loved one who has died. *This can't be happening. I can't believe it. It must have happened to someone else. I know I'm going to wake up and it will just be a dream, a nightmare. I know they are dead, but I just can't believe it.* This concept of Denial was revised much later in *On Grief and Grieving – Finding the Meaning of Grief Through the Five Stages of Loss* by Elisabeth Kübler-Ross and co-author David Kessler. In this book, it states, 'The denial is still not denial of the actual death, even though someone may be saying, "I can't believe he's dead." The person is actually saying this, at first, because it is too much for his or her psyche'.

In 2005, my nephew, Ryan, died tragically at the very young age of 19 years. I well remember my daughter, Jessica, saying, 'Could it be another Ryan who's died? I mean, there are many people that have the same name, maybe it's someone else.' The shock of what had happened was just too much to hold in her mind. She was not alone in this.

This stage, therefore, can act like a buffer, helping to protect us from the full force of the intense and overwhelming pain. As it states eloquently in *On Grief and Grieving*, 'It is nature's way of letting in only as much as we can handle.'

This is one of the reasons it may be helpful to view the body, wherever possible, because it helps us to actually *know*, at a deep level, what has happened, that this person has died, and it's not someone else. Difficulty often arises when a body is not found and we may struggle for years, consciously and/or unconsciously, searching for the person who has died. This makes for lengthy and complex bereavement as we may never truly believe or accept that our loved one has actually died.

There may be moments when you think that your loved one is about to walk through the door. It's as though you can hold two concepts in your mind at the same time, dead and not dead. I remember my mum looking for Dad during the night, asking where he slept because she knew that he couldn't have slept with her in a single bed. When I put my arms around her and said, 'Mum, Dad died,' she replied very clearly, 'Yes I know he died, but he must be asleep somewhere. I was dreaming.' And indeed she was well aware that it was a dream. She knew he was dead, yet it was still logical to look for him.

Also, I think that death, for most of us, is such a difficult concept to get our head around. The concept of 'not there' is so unbelievable. Knowing that you will never see the person again is just totally foreign to us and very difficult to comprehend.

Eventually reality does begin to seep into our being. And as this happens, although it may not seem like it, we are already on the road to healing. It doesn't feel like healing, of course, because as the buffer of denial gradually falls away, the rawness of what has happened comes to the surface and a whole gamut of emotions and thoughts come bubbling to the surface.

ANGER

Anger can be anger about literally anything. It may manifest itself as *Why did God do this to me? Why did this have to happen?* Anger at the person who has died. Anger at a relative who did not die, *Why was it my child and not my parent? They are old and it wouldn't have mattered so much.* Anger at doctors who should have done more. Some years ago my little dog died and I was terribly angry at the vet who had attended her, who I was sure should and could have done more, should have referred her to a specialist earlier.

Anger may also be directed at a friend or a family member, *Why did my child die and not yours?* Reading this you may think, *I would never think that, that's a horrible thing to think*, but when we are bereaved our thoughts are not ordered, not logical and we need to be very accepting and forgiving of ourselves at this time.

Anger at yourself for not being able to do more is also a common expression of grief. *I should have done more. I should have spent more time with them. I should not have had that argument. I should not have...* and so it goes on. The close cousin of anger is guilt. I will talk more about guilt later on.

Of course, beneath anger lurks deep pain, the agony. In a sense, anger is the buffer for pain, because the pain may be too difficult to go near. The pain knows no bounds and is a bottomless pit, too scary to be fully immersed in. Anger becomes a safer emotion than the despair and anguish. Anger gives us something to focus on.

It may be difficult for loved ones to understand, as an expression of anger is often frowned upon in families, and others may be dealing with their own feelings of anguish and feelings of anger and guilt.

Anger at this system we call life, the unfairness of it all, is also not uncommon. Anger at God may call us to question whether there really is a God, because after all, what sort of a God would do this. It feels like God has somehow vacated the scene. Our spirituality may be shifted to one side or we may indeed decide that it's all rubbish. I had first hand experience of this when Ryan died, as I thought to myself...*It* (spirituality/God) *is all just a crock of crap*. My spirituality, a very important part of me, just simply vanished, and there was a time when I thought that I was probably done with it. However, I was also aware that I was in shock, and so I decided to 'shelve' any major decisions regarding my spiritual beliefs (along with any other decisions) for later. Actually, all these feelings that surface are at the very core, the very centre of the healing process. But, it doesn't feel like it at the time.

I am reminded of a beautiful poem called 'Footprints In The Sand'. Even if you have already read this, it's worth another look...

One night a man had a dream. He dreamed he was walking along the beach with the LORD. Across the sky flashed scenes from his life. For each scene he noticed two sets of footprints in the sand. One belonging to him and the other to the LORD.

When the last scene of his life flashed before him, he looked back at the footprints in the sand. He noticed that many times along the path of his life there was only one set of footprints. He also noticed that it happened at the very lowest and saddest times of his life.

This really bothered him and he questioned the LORD about it. 'Lord, you said that once I decided to follow you, you'd walk with me all the way. But I have noticed that during the most

troublesome times in my life there is only one set of footprints.
I don't understand why when I needed
you most you would leave me.'

The LORD replied, 'My precious, precious child, I love you
and I would never leave you! During your times of trial and suf-
fering when you saw only one set of footprints,
it was then that I carried you.'

Footprints in the Sand – Carolyn Carty

This makes me cry each and every time I read it, and beautifully highlights that intense feeling that we are walking alone in our grief, when in actual fact it is at these moments we are being carried.

It is important to remember that anger may surface, disappear and resurface many times over years. 'Time is a great healer' is a common enough saying, but grief does not play the game of time. David's (my husband) mother died of breast cancer when he was six years old, and every now and then the sadness will still touch him at the most unexpected time, creeping up sneakily. Grief creeps up on us when we least expect it, and whacks us from behind, and anger can also be a part of this.

If you are experiencing anger as a part of grief at this moment in your life it may be helpful to know that this is quite normal. It may also be helpful to find a way to express your anger in a safe way. Locking the doors to your home, when no one is around, and screaming is one such way. Running, swimming, or any physical exercise may also be helpful at this time. Find someone, a friend, counsellor, or therapist who will listen without judgment. Find verbal expression of the anger.

It is important to differentiate between anger and violence. No one has the right to harm another. Anger is one thing; aggression and violence are something quite different. Generally speaking, grief and bereavement do not make a person violent. If a person demonstrates violence then it was probably already there to begin with. Anger is a normal, natural reaction to an injustice.

Accept your anger, you cannot hide from it, nor should you. It needs to be acknowledged and expressed in a safe environment. Finding someone you can trust, a non-judgmental friend, a grief counsellor, can make the world of difference.

BARGAINING

The bargaining 'stage' of grief is when we begin to bargain for what we are about to lose if our loved one is nearing death, or have lost if they have already died. Making pacts or bargaining with God is common. We may say, 'I will do anything if you just let my child live.' This is also the stage where the 'what ifs' start to creep in, and we may find ourselves immersed in a barrage of them. 'If only I could have made the doctors work more quickly, if only I could have stopped the accident, if only, if only, if only...'

And again, guilt is also the cousin to bargaining, as we start to blame ourselves for not being good enough, not being smart enough, not being able to stop what happened. We would do anything to prevent this from happening.

In a way this stage is about letting more of the pain in, as we begin to acknowledge what has happened. We think that we may somehow be able to reverse what has happened.

DEPRESSION

I was speaking with a friend a few days ago and she was relating to me what it was like for her after her father died. Months after he died she came to the realisation that she was depressed. She felt flat, sad, unmotivated and so forth, and had been for some time. Wondering what was wrong, she went to her doctor who prescribed anti-depressants. Now, my friend definitely did not want to take anti-depressants and so she started to look for alternatives, wondering what this uncomfortable feeling was all about. In her search, she found a book on grief, and was just amazed to discover that what she was feeling, depressed, was a normal part of grief. She had not associated her 'flat' feeling with the loss of her dad, because in her mind she should be over it by now.

Depression may set in months after a death and may come unbidden and unexpected. It may take us some time to even recognise that we are depressed. It may be a continuum from other stages of grief or it may come in isolation. As I have stressed earlier, there is no correct way, and each stage appears to have a life of its own. Depression is a perfectly normal natural reaction to loss. Once my friend became aware that what she was feeling was very normal, she could then acknowledge it, understand it, and take care of herself, nurture herself and wait for it to pass.

Depression incorporates feelings of not really caring what is happening, feeling flat, unmotivated, nothing really matters anymore. The feelings are dark. It's what my mum has labelled 'The Miseries'. You may question, *Why bother getting out of bed, why bother eating, why bother socialising, why bother...?* Like the boy with no Shadow questioning, *What is the point?* Life begins to lose its meaning for us, and things that were important to us may no longer seem that way.

Depression happens when we are hurting at a soul level. Someone once said, 'Depression is like a cocoon that we weave around ourselves when things are just too much to bear.' And I think this is an apt description, as depression gives us a break; it is nature's way of closing down for a while to give us a rest from the trauma of grief.

When depression pays a visit the further away from it we try to run, the faster it follows in our wake. There is no escape. Antidepressants may numb us, but it's like placing a band-aid over a wound – it will eventually fester unless it is properly cleaned and dressed. And so it is with depression. When we experience loss and we feel depressed we need to firstly acknowledge it, welcome it...it means you are *normal*. Accept that this is how it is for you right now. Seeking a grief counsellor can be of help, but understanding that this is a normal, natural part of grief is often all that is needed. Nurture yourself, take extra care. If you broke your leg, what would you do? You'd rest it, nurture it, take the pressure off for a while to give your body's natural healing mechanisms a chance to kick in. If depression becomes a destructive force in your life and you are not coping, then the doctor is your first port of call. Anti-depressants may well help you to cope a little better with life, but more often depression is a call from the soul to nurture yourself.

ACCEPTANCE

Acceptance does not mean that what has happened, or is happening, is okay. It does not make everything better or mean that you are over the loss. The truth is that you may never be over the loss, but you can begin to accept what has happened; you can begin to 'accommodate' the loss in some way within your mind and within your life. In other words, you know it has happened, it is painful, you know how much it hurts, *and* you are also beginning to find some meaning to your life.

If 'accommodate' or 'acceptance' was a painting I would see it as a special place, a pocket, within the heart where the pain is stored, there to be accessed when needed, ready to move to the fore, either bidden or unbidden. It is often when we begin to find this 'pocket' in which to accommodate our pain that we truly begin to pick up the pieces and re-enter life.

It may be at this point that we begin to form a new relationship with the person who has died; however, it will never be quite the same again and everything has changed. We may begin to accept that this has happened; begin to re-engage and re-connect with our loved one, and to accept that this relationship is now different.

When my dad died, I couldn't look at a photo of him, because it felt like someone was sticking a knife into me. This was hard because Mum would constantly have the family albums out and say to me, 'Look at this photo. That's you and your dad.' And I got very good at 'looking' but not 'seeing' the photos. It was just too hard. And the not 'seeing' was like a steel wall coming down in my mind. I simply did not see, a part of my mind shut down. Eventually I started seeing, just a glimpse of a photo as I walked past one. I would just test if it was okay for me to look, each time knowing it was going to hurt like hell. And so the steel shutter eventually began to rise. I was beginning to 'accept' or 'accommodate', in my own way, in my own time, at my own pace. Little by little, allowing it to come in. Months later and I am still in the process of only allowing so much in at any one time. I still can only look at any one photo for so long. I know my limit.

With acceptance we begin to re-join life, friends, work and so forth. Sometimes acceptance just creeps up on us. There are good days and bad days, and the further down the track we get the more good days we may experience. The bad days will also be lurking, not too far out of sight. Guilt may also resurface as we begin to rejoin life, and we may have feelings that it isn't okay for us to have a nice time, to laugh, to share a coffee with a friend or go shopping. Again this is all normal.

NORMAL GRIEF REACTIONS

Here are some other normal grief reactions and experiences we may have:

- Loneliness.
- Fatigue. This may or may not be related to poor sleep patterns.
- Feelings of helplessness.
- Shock.
- Disbelief.
- Brain fog. Difficulty remembering the simplest things.
- Difficulty sleeping. Over sleeping. Difficulty getting out of bed.
- A need to withdraw from social activities.
- Not eating or overeating.
- Looking for the person who has died.
- Anxiety.

- Feelings of guilt. I should have…I could have…etc
- Body tension.
- Hyperactivity.
- Lethargy.
- Feelings of wanting to die.
- Nightmares.
- Feelings of fear. Sometimes not even knowing why we feel scared.
- Feelings of relief, particularly if the person who has died has been sick for a long period of time.
- Feeling like you've stepped into a nightmare.
- Increased or decreased libido and sexual activity.
- Feelings of unreality. This is part of shock.
- Manifesting bodily symptoms of the person who has died. For example when a man dies of a heart attack his wife may experience chest pain. When checked out by a doctor there are no signs of heart problems. This may recur at anniversaries and at other special times. (If you have any bodily symptoms these should always be checked out by your doctor.)

One of the things that may happen when we are bereaved is that we regress in age. This can last for some time and may manifest itself in many ways. We tend to become a younger version of ourselves. According to one of Australia's leading experts on grief and bereavement, Mal McKissock, adults may regress to somewhere between seven and fourteen years of age, but sometimes younger. We may find ourselves behaving like we did when we were teenagers. If we were socially withdrawn during our teens then we may withdraw from our social environment. It's as if we just step back in time. This is perfectly normal. What you need to keep in mind is that other family members who are bereaved will more than likely do the same. You can imagine what havoc this creates in families.

This is also true of children. Children may begin to bed wet, throw tantrums, become 'clingy' and basically regress to a younger age. This is all perfectly normal. If you are regressed yourself you may find this difficult to cope with. It's easy to snap, smack and get angry with them. Don't. Remember these little people are hurting also. It's a difficult time. If you need a break, ask a friend to look after your kids for a while. Above all, your kids need extra love and understanding.

The important thing to remember is that our reactions to bereavement are all normal, natural ways in which we cope with the chaos of our loss. Each of the stages takes its time. The word *stage* implies that we will move through each phase in a sequential and logical manner. But as I have previously outlined, this is not so. I think the words 'state' or 'reaction' could be substituted for the word 'stage' as it pays tribute to the impermanent and transient nature of grief. We can all relate to this. We may feel happy, sad, angry, peaceful, and these states flow through us and from us daily. They are non-static and do not come in any particular order. So it is with reactions of grief. We may become stuck in one state, skip another altogether, visit and revisit a state many times. No state can be forced and we may experience a barrage of other things along the way. There is no uniform way to 'do' grief. However, if you feel stuck *do seek help*.

As we have already seen, the Five Stages of Grief — denial, anger, bargaining, depression and acceptance — are phases that we may experience when we lose someone whom we love. They are all intrinsically *human* experiences; at the same time they are unique to each individual. There is no agenda and grief does not follow any particular course or set pattern. Grief does its own thing in its own time.

BREATHING PEACE

This simple exercise will lay the foundation for re-connecting with your loved one and for other activities throughout this book.

Breathing is something that we do all day (and night) long, and yet rarely do we pay attention to it. Breathing is an integral part of many spiritual practices; it brings energy into balance and restores vitality to the body.

So take the phone off the hook to ensure you are not disturbed and begin wherever you are right now. You do not need to be lying down, sitting is just fine.

Close your eyes over lightly as you take in a nice deep breath, and as you do so just imagine breathing peace into your heart. I don't know what colour peace is for you, but just notice now the colour of peace. Imagine it entering each chamber, filling your heart's centre with the colour of peace.

Allow any pain held within to gently soften around the edges.

And breathe out slowly.

Breathing in once more allowing the colour of peace now to wash gently into your mind. Lapping softly at the shores of your consciousness. Taking the colour of peace into your mind.

And breathe out.

Breathing in, take the colour of peace into your belly this time. Allowing any pain stored within your belly to soften. Just notice the colour of peace within your belly.

And breathe out.

Now take another breath in, this time taking the colour of peace into your whole body. Notice as any tight spots begin to soften as the colour of peace enfolds your being.

And breathe out.

When you are ready just open your eyes and bring your awareness back into the room.

Make a commitment to yourself to practise this mini meditation daily. It need only take a few moments. Instead of 'peace', you might like to incorporate some other states such as 'love' or 'calm'. Find what best works for you.

Record your experiences in your journal. Whilst doing this consider the following:

What colour was the colour of peace for you?

Did the colour of peace change in any areas of your body or did it stay the same?

What feelings were associated with the colour of peace?

What emotions surfaced during this meditation?

What thoughts or memories arose in your mind?

Record anything else you think may be relevant.

Two

LETTING GO

The shadow of your smile when you have gone,
Will colour all my dreams and light the dawn...

The Shadow of Your Smile

Johnny Mandel and Paul Francis Webster

'People keep telling me I have to let go. I have all my son's clothes washed and neatly pressed in the cupboard and I know I need to clear them all out, get rid of them. All the boxes filled with his stuff. But I just can't bear the thought of throwing anything away. I know I have to let go, I have to move on.'

'Whoever is telling you this has the very best intentions for you. But they are wrong. You don't ever have to let go. He's your son! Why would you ever want to let go? Those things can sit in your cupboard for the rest of your life and it's okay. He's your son! Don't ever let go.'

This conversation took place between a family member and myself four years after her son died. The agony of contemplating 'letting go' is unbearable. Society, and our friends, dictate that we 'move on' that we 'let go' and have 'closure'. And yet we know in our hearts, in every fibre of our being, that this is wrong. We know it at a soul level. It's instinctive. This is why four years have now passed and her son's things are neatly folded and pressed and put away. Society, and indeed our friends, have a lot to answer for! The contemplation of moving on, of letting go, creates agony, because we are being asked to do something that is against what we know to be right.

Letting go. Two little words that haunt many who have lost someone they hold most dear in their heart. Why? Why would anyone ever want to let go of their son, or their daughter, or their husband, or their lover?

When someone we love has died, that moment of letting go may never come in this lifetime. You may never ever want to let go. And this is okay. Letting go does not mean that you like what has happened. It does not mean that you wouldn't give the world to change it if you could. It does not mean that you don't miss the person. It does not mean that you don't hurt like hell. Letting go certainly does not mean throwing away your loved one's possessions, or that you are ready to move on.

What about 'holding on'? What if you hold on, as opposed to let go, to the relationship you have with your loved one who has died? What will happen? Will you still function in the world? Can you still hold relationships in the physical world? Of course you can. Just because you hold onto a relationship with someone who has died does not mean that you have to ignore other earthly relationships. If I talk to one person it doesn't mean I have to ignore someone else.

In a sense, the act of resolving to hold on, rather than let go, is a letting go in itself. It is letting go of what we think we 'should' be doing, or what others think we 'should' be doing. Some years ago a client came to see me. This client presented to me with feelings of overwhelming sadness, but had absolutely no idea why she felt this way. She said that she could be out shopping, or at work, or doing almost anything and this feeling of sadness would simply 'hit' her and she would be in floods of tears. So as we talked for a while, there seemed to be nothing untoward that would cause such a reaction. She was happily married with three grownup children, also happily married. All seemed rosy in the garden. She was baffled by it and so was I. Under hypnosis, however, it was a very different story.

I use a form of regression which allows the client to access subconscious (below the level of conscious awareness) memories and perceptions. Without getting too technical, I asked this client's subconscious mind to take her back to the time when this sadness was first present. 'Oh, no,' she said, 'It can't be that!' dismissing the images of what she was seeing and feeling. And there it was, only a blackness at first, a 'foggy' area. But she knew what it was. During her early years of marriage she had had two miscarriages, before finally having three beautiful children. Through this time, she had never once allowed herself to grieve in any way whatsoever. She had literally dismissed the entire episode. She had 'pulled herself together' and got on with it.

Whenever we actively 'force' ourselves to 'let go' or to pull ourselves together, we are *dismissing* our grief, along with the person who has died. Ignoring our grief is like holding a beach ball under water. You can't do it forever and eventually it will fly up and hit you in the face. All the grief, the loss, the sadness, along with a two small babies, were still clinging tightly to this client. And this is how it is. Letting go is not something you can force. It's like grasping double-sided sticky-tape; you pull it off one hand only to find it is stuck firmly to the other. This is what happens when we try to 'let go' or dismiss grief. It stays stuck.

If anyone tells you it's time to 'let go', just know that they may have the very best intentions for your wellbeing; however, they are wrong. It is not uncommon for people to tell you it's time to clear out deceased loved one's clothes, possessions and so forth, so you can 'move on'. Crap! – there is simply no other word for it. Don't have a bar of it.

When someone we love has died, letting go, if it is going to happen, needs to happen naturally, and when it does you can be sure it is just the right moment. Letting go should not be forced in any way and has nothing whatsoever to do with throwing anything away. It is important to understand that we are all unique individuals and for this reason letting go will be different for each and every one of us. For some people, letting go is simply not an option. For some, it may happen in an instant, in the blink of an eye. For others, letting go may take years, a slow release. Celebrate your uniqueness and allow yourself the luxury of being who you are. And for the time being, at least, settle down and make a decision to never let go.

PERMISSION

Read each of the following statements then close your eyes and say them silently to yourself. Notice if anything resonates within you. If it does and it feels like a weight has been lifted then write it in big letters and keep it on your fridge. Say it to yourself like a mantra at every opportunity.

Conversely, if any press buttons within you, causing you to feel uncomfortable feelings such as anger, sadness, fear or guilt, then know that this is an area that may need some work at some stage - when you are ready.

I give myself permission to grieve in my own way.

I give myself permission to cry/not cry.

I give myself permission to accept all of my feelings.

I give myself permission to be angry.

I give myself permission to sit and do nothing.

I give myself permission to love myself.

I give myself permission to forgive. If you have difficulty with this one you aren't the only one – forgiving someone is hard, forgiving yourself is harder. Good therapy can make all the difference when the time is right. If this is difficult for you right now try – I give myself permission to *accept* that I don't forgive.

I give myself permission to stay awake all night and sleep all day.

I give myself permission to talk about what has happened.

I give myself permission to go into exile for a time.

I give myself permission to withdraw from social events.

I give myself permission to 'take a break' from grief.

I give myself permission to go out and enjoy myself.

I give myself permission to allow joy into my life.

I give myself permission to be spiritual.

I give myself permission to talk to my loved one.

I give myself permission to (you put your own ending on it).

Make a record in your journal of which 'permissions' sat comfortably with you and which did not. What reactions did they provoke in you as you said them to yourself? Repeat this exercise again in one month, six months and then again in twelve months' time. Notice if there are any changes in your reactions.

Three

TOOLS FOR THE BEREAVED

Beautiful...

Elizabeth Barrett Browning
(on being asked how she felt moments before she died)

I f you are newly bereaved, and you are reading this, I know that you are already beginning to take care of yourself, beginning to cope. Here are some things that may help you at this time.

BE ACCEPTING OF YOURSELF

This is probably one of the most difficult times you have ever had to face. Look after yourself. Do whatever feels right to relieve the unbearable feelings. Crying is normal. Not crying is also quite normal.

Grief reactions widely vary from person to person, just because someone does not cry does not mean that they are not grieving. They are. They just express it differently. If you are not a cryer, then just accept this. It means you are normal!

DON'T MAKE ANY MAJOR DECISIONS

Unless absolutely necessary, shelve any major decisions for a good couple of years. There is no hurry, take your time. You will know what to do once the time is right. As I write this I can hear my dad's voice in my ear, 'If you don't know what to do, do nothing.' One of his little pearls of wisdom.

DEVELOP A SUPPORT NETWORK

When we are newly bereaved friends and family gather in droves. When my dad died my house looked like a florist shop and I almost considered putting a revolving door at the front of my house as so many people made their pilgrimage to visit. Usually after about six or seven weeks have passed, everybody vanishes and you are finally left alone with your grief. Now, what can happen at this point is that we tend then to rely on one or two close family members or friends for emotional support, someone to lean on at those times when we feel most bereft. We may need this for quite some time, but the truth is that shouldering someone in this way is hard work. If it is falling to only one person it becomes a burden. It is important, therefore, to think about having a network of support people, rather than leaving it to just one or two. Make a list of people who may be willing to assist. Ask them outright if they are willing to help out, don't wait for them to offer. It has been said that someone will go out of their way to avoid a person who is bereaved, and I think this is quite true. I remember a close friend of mine commenting that not one of her friends ever bothered to call her in the six months following their initial acknowledgments of her husband's death. This is partly because people just don't know what to say or do and so they hope that it will somehow all disappear if they just ignore it. They may feel helpless to take away your pain. They also get busy with their own lives and forget that your world has been shattered. So get yourself a network of people you can call on occasionally. It may be that you only call on them once or twice a month, but it just gives your main support a break.

When we are bereaved we may have a need to talk about what has happened. We may need to do this frequently. It's like we are trying to understand what has happened to us and we will keep on repeating the same story over and over, telling and retelling it in a never ending fashion. This is quite normal, but family members and friends may get sick of hearing it. Bereavement counselling may be of benefit here as it gives you the opportunity to tell your story, to get it out in all its minute detail and do it all again at the following session if you need to. Actually it is very important that you do keep talking about it as each time you do you are actually coming to terms with the shock of what has happened. It's all a normal and natural part of the journey.

DISTRACT YOURSELF

When we are bereaved it can be daunting if we have too much time on our hands. Being alone and bereaved can be the pits. Make a list of things you can do to distract yourself for a while. It might include things like going for a walk, cleaning out a cupboard, hiring movies, going to the movies, calling a friend (as long as it's not the same friend you called five minutes ago), meeting someone for coffee, or perhaps a hobby. Make a list and keep it handy so you can glance at it periodically to give you inspiration. Initially when you begin to 'do' all the pain will go with you, but eventually it will get easier and serve to give you a short break from the full brunt of it.

Make Time to Do Simple Self-Nurturing Exercises

As already suggested, take the time to do the simple exercises at the end of each chapter. If at any time something does not feel comfortable for you, stop. Maybe it's not the right moment or the right environment for you to be doing this. Respect how you feel.

Get yourself a journal and begin to record your experiences as you do the exercises.

Be Aware That Everyone Grieves Differently

Every single person will show their grief in different ways. No two people will experience bereavement in exactly the same way. It is as individual as a fingerprint. However, it is important to understand that men and women may express their grief in different ways. Women tend to talk, cry, share and immerse themselves in their feelings, whereas men tend to immerse themselves in their work. It does not mean that one is grieving any more than the other. It's just simply a different way of expressing it. What may catch us out is that women can often mistake this for not caring, not grieving, when in fact quite the opposite is true. Conversely, men may perceive their partners as not coping because they are crying lots, they don't have the dinner on the table when they get home and the house is a mess. This disparity can sometimes be devastating to a relationship. But just know that you are both grieving, you are just doing it differently. That's all.

Don't Force Letting Go

Letting go may happen, it may not. There is no 'got to' about it. Do what feels most comfortable to you.

UNLOCKING THE MIND

When my nephew, Ryan, died I was deeply afraid, and this overwhelming fear continued for weeks. The overriding emotions were shock, horror, terror and fear, melded together with grief and pain. There was a tight ball of mass that was my grief enmeshed within my psyche and I was held tightly in its clutches. This manifested itself in what is known as night terrors. I would wake up in the middle of the night in a cold sweat, absolutely terrified. Not only did I have to put *all* the lights in the bedroom on, but my husband, David, also had to be awake. I was frantic. And the thing that really bugged me was that I had no idea what was frightening me so much. It was below my conscious level of awareness. Sleeping was a nightmare, literally.

There is a wonderful technique that I have developed, originally derived from NLP (Neuro Linguistic Programming), that I often employ with clients in my own practice. It allows us to unlock the mind and to crystallise the essence of an issue while facilitating internal resolution, often without the client even realising what is going on. It's called Parts Integration, and is not specifically used in the area of grief, but I found it beneficial with my own night terrors and the shock and horror when Ryan died. It gave me clarity on what was frightening me. Once I was aware of it, whilst it still upset me, I was no longer waking in abject fear.

Here's what I did. I held my hands out in front of my body and I invited my uncomfortable feelings to step forward and sit on one of my hands. I was scared, but I had to know what it was, because not knowing was more scary than knowing. Ignorance breeds fear. The image that immediately popped into my head, and subsequently out onto my hand, was a giant ball of spaghetti. So I sat with this ball of spaghetti on my hand and I simply asked it what it was. As this happened it began to unravel, quite by its own volition, to separate into individual strands and to lay itself strand by strand across my arm.

I knew that in my brain the mash of emotions was beginning to unravel and perhaps I could now begin to at last understand my 'head mess'. I watched as this unfolded, amazed at what the mind is capable of.

As I looked, wondering what was going to happen next, there was one strand that stood out from all the rest. That strand was fear. So I asked, *What is this fear about?*

And there it was. Spaghetti unravelled, the penny dropped. What I had been most afraid of, unconsciously, was particular aspects regarding Ryan's death that I had not consciously acknowledged or thought about. My unconscious mind was telling a story all of its own. Even now as I write this, the tears stream. It is unbearable.

But buried in my subconscious, it was wreaking havoc inside my head. Out in the open at least I could openly acknowledge it, openly grieve it. Hidden away in the mish-mash of mess I could not even begin to understand it. It had me in its grip. Interestingly, once I knew what it was, I did not wake up again with night terrors and I felt much clearer in my head, as if somehow the jumble that was in there had been cleaned up.

This particular exercise can work well with either a jumble of emotions or with a single uncomfortable feeling such as anxiety. I use it in my practice with a variety of issues, including anxiety, depression and smoking, weight loss and of course grief. It allows you to *begin* to process *stuff* inside your head. It will not take away your grief. No one can do this. There is no magic wand here. If you feel comfortable doing it alone, this is fine. Alternatively a friend can assist you.

If you feel uncomfortable at any time, respect this is how it is for you right now and stop. Do not continue with any exercise if you feel uncomfortable. I recommend you see a therapist with whom you feel comfortable, if you feel it is more appropriate for you.

Find a comfortable place to sit and begin by Breathing Peace for a few moments.

Hold your hands at right angles to your body, palms facing upwards, elbows tucked into your waist.

Invite the uncomfortable feeling to sit forward on one of your hands. I don't know which hand it will sit on, but it is normal and natural that it will want to do so.

Once you feel it sitting on your hand, notice what shape the uncomfortable feeling takes the form of. Notice whether it is big or small, and any colour that is associated with it. Notice if it reminds you of anything or anyone. This could be a person or an object or symbol or it could be metaphorical, like spaghetti.

Whilst you may not understand what its purpose is for you, most parts of us are just trying to protect us in some way. Sometimes the behaviour generated from this is counter-productive for us, but the part is still just doing its best to protect us. Hidden away, my uncomfortable feelings were wreaking havoc, but protecting me initially from thoughts that were just too hard for me to bear. My brain had simply forgotten to release this information into my conscious mind so it could be processed and acknowledged. Hidden away it festered and grew like fungus.

So, just say *thank you* to this part of you that is sitting on your hand. Now notice what it does. Often a part will begin to shrink (or unravel like spaghetti). This is because we are acknowledging the uncomfortable feeling rather than trying to get away from it.

Whatever this part of you does, just thank it again and notice what it does.

Keep thanking and noticing until it feels appropriate to stop. You will know when this is. It's instinctive.

Now go inside your mind and find the opposite part to this part that is now sitting on your hand. The opposite part might be 'peace' or it might be 'joy' or 'nurturing' or it might be some higher part of yourself that is infinitely wise, infinitely healing. Now invite this part of yourself to also come forward and to sit on your other hand.

Notice too any colours or sounds or shapes associated with this part of you. Notice if it reminds you of anyone you know.

Ask this part of you that is infinitely wise to share its wisdom with this other part that is struggling on your other hand.

Allow your hands to turn and to face each other. Bring your hands together only as quickly or as slowly as this wise part of you is willing to share its knowledge and its wisdom with this other part of you. Because this wise part has the key, and there is a natural pull to be whole. Allow a sharing, a free flow of peace and wisdom. Take your time.

When your hands have come together, just allow them to be drawn to a part of your body that feels most appropriate. For some this is the chest, the heart centre. For some it is the belly. Wherever it is for you, just allow your hands to be drawn to this part of your body and allow these two parts of you to go wherever they need to go.

Take a deep breath and know that these two parts can continue to share for as long as they need to, each assisting the other in infinite ways, a sharing of wisdom and knowledge and healing.

QUICK REFERENCE GUIDE

1. Hold your arms at right angles to your body, with your palms facing upwards.

2. Invite the uncomfortable feeling to come and sit on one of your hands.

3. Notice what this part looks like, feels like, and anything else associated with this part.

4. Thank this part and notice what it does. Continue until it feels appropriate to stop.

5. Now go inside your mind and find the opposite part, this may be a wise part of yourself, or it might be joy or love or some other part that is willing to help.

6. Notice what this part looks like.

7. Ask this part to share its wisdom with the other part (the uncomfortable feeling) that is sitting on your other hand.

8. Turn your hands to face each other and allow a sharing of wisdom between these two parts.

9. Bring your hands together only as quickly as the part that is wise is willing to share its wisdom, knowledge and understanding with the uncomfortable part.

10. Take a deep breath and allow your hands to go to some part of your body where they feel drawn to, allowing these two parts to go where they need to go.

Record what took place within your journal.

Four

TOOLS FOR THE
SUPPORT PERSON

A ship exists on the ocean, even if it sails out beyond the limits of our sight. The people in the ship have not vanished; they are simply moving to another shore.

On Grief and Grieving

Elizabeth Kübler-Ross and David Kessler

B eing a support person for someone who is dying or bereaved is a challenging role indeed. At times you may feel overwhelmed by your role. At other times you may feel as though you are doing nothing and feelings of inadequacy may run riot.

Here are some things to remember.

GRIEF IS NORMAL

All of the Five Stages of Grief and dying are a normal, natural part of grief and bereavement and the dying journey, and may last for many months and even years. Because someone is grieving and passing though these phases in their own way at their own time does not mean that they are not coping. Most people cope in some fashion. If it has been two years since the death and they are still crying, feeling angry or guilty and so forth, they *are* coping. They are just feeling sad or angry or guilty. But they are coping.

The Five Stages of Grief are just as relevant to someone who is dying as they are to the person who is experiencing grief. The knowledge of the loss of our own life is, in itself, a grief. Big time. Denial, anger, bargaining, depression and acceptance are all states that we may pass through on this journey into death. In the last couple of years in my dad's life many a conversation was had regarding his trip. He did not want to go, as most of us don't. Denial, manifested in not taking care of any affairs such as making wills, what he wanted to happen to assets and so forth, how Mum would be taken care of etc. Anxiety then ran riot, resulting in several wills being made and subsequently destroyed within a very short time frame, much to the delight of the solicitor. Eruptions of anger were common place. And when anger was just too hard to manage, depression would ensue.

Which brings us to the next point.

GROW THICKER SKIN!

Don't take anger stages personally. Think: *like water off a duck's back*!

TREAD GENTLY

These are difficult times for both of you.

DON'T TRY TO SOLVE IT

You can't. Feelings of helplessness are normal if you are a support person for either someone who is dying or bereaved. You want to do *something*. If you feel helpless, get used to it – just be still, don't try to fix everything. Do not underestimate your presence. As a support person you are helping far more than you will ever know.

TALK ABOUT IMPORTANT ISSUES

One of the most difficult issues to talk about with a loved one is death. If it is a friend who is dying it is no less easy. Concern about saying the wrong thing leads to ignoring what *is*, pretending *it* isn't happening. Opening up a conversation to invite your loved one to talk about death is never an easy thing to do. Offering the opportunity to talk about what is happening needs to be simple and clear, *I'm feeling really sad about what's happening, I'm wondering what you must be feeling?* Avoid asking, *How are you feeling?* as this will often lead to a monosyllabic, tight lipped *Fine*. Saying *I'm really scared…* and leaving the sentence unfinished can also be a way of gently letting them know it's okay to talk.

Not saying anything is a missed opportunity; an opportunity to allow you to be closer to each other, to share in something very special, to let them know that you do care, you do love them, will miss them. It also gives space for them to talk about what is going on for them.

When someone is bereaved they often have a great need to tell and retell the story of the death, the funeral and the many aspects of the life they have shared with the person who has died. This can go on for months, sometimes longer. This is normal and natural. It may seem to you, the support person, that they are telling you the same thing over and over again. Firstly, this is part of coming to terms with what has happened. Going over and over what has happened allows their brain to begin to *accept*. Secondly, the story, whilst sounding the same, will actually be slightly different each time they tell it. The bereaved person will have times when their dialogue drifts into past happy times, and then will come abruptly back to the 'now' moment. This is a very important part of the healing journey. When someone we love first dies we are immersed in the shock of what has happened. Nothing outside of this event exists. Nothing. Then slowly, slowly we begin to talk about the happy times we have had with the person who has died. This is actually the beginnings of re-establishing the link, the reconnection with the person who has died. We look at this in much more detail in Part 4 of this book. It is important that the bereaved person does this. As a support person this can be frustrating and we may perceive the person as 'not coping'. In actual fact they *are* coping, beautifully. They are reorganising their relationship. Bereaved people often do this quite naturally. It allows them to escape from the 'dead' person and re-engage with the 'living' person. It is comforting as they begin to re-connect with what they think they have lost.

If the person who has died was sick or incapacitated for a protracted length of time before dying, it may be difficult for the bereaved person to access memories of past happy events. They will often only be able to focus on the illness and how difficult things were during this time. It can be useful to ask them about specific events, for example, if it is a spouse that has died you could ask about what it was like when they first met. Talking about specific memories such as the birth of the first child is a way of linking the person back in with good memories rather than just the illness in the preceding months before death.

At some point they will eventually start to talk about the future without the person who has died. This is also a normal and natural progression.

LISTEN MORE, TALK LESS

Listen with your heart, not with your mouth. Allow the person who is bereaved or is dying to have the space to talk about what is happening for them. Sometimes they just need to 'off load'.

I well remember sitting with my dad when a whole monologue of 'stuff' bubbled forth about the prospects of his death. It went on for quite some time and I sat and just listened. When he drew breath I simply said, 'Dad, it's *really* scary.' 'YES!' came back his response. He would often say, 'I feel so much better when I talk to you.' All I did was listen. Listening is one of the most powerful tools you can have.

Trying to solve anything is unhelpful because you can't. Resist the urge to say things like, 'Don't be silly,' or, 'Pull yourself together,' or 'Stop whingeing.' Don't try changing the subject either. Don't say, 'I know how you feel,' because the truth is, you don't. No one does. No one can ever really understand how someone feels because this is a subjective experience. The inner world of someone else's grief is something that only they can truly know.

BE PRESENT

Being present for someone who is dying or is bereaved can be one of the most special things you can do. Often, it is all you can do. Your presence is all that is required.

REMEMBER SPECIAL OCCASIONS

Don't forget anniversaries, birthdays and Christmas. These times can be especially difficult for someone who is bereaved. A phone call or even a card at these times can be special and lets them know that they are not forgotten and nor have you forgotten the person who has died. Be sensitive; if this is not appreciated then make sure you respect this. Not everyone appreciates being reminded. I once sent a card to my brother on the anniversary of his son's death, just letting him know that I was thinking of him. He asked me not to do it again. I respect his wishes, and now only make sure that I call him around this time. I do not mention his son, but the call lets him know I care, without actually bringing it out in the open.

ERADICATE THE 'POOR YOU' ATTITUDE FROM YOUR MIND

People are enormously resourceful and it is important to keep this in mind. Pity is usually not appreciated. But at the same time, be ready to offer practical help where necessary. This can be as simple as cooking a meal, mowing the lawns or going out for a coffee with them. If you are unsure, ask them how you can best support them.

LOOK AFTER YOURSELF

Take time out to give yourself a break. And do it often. Schedule it in. Do something nice for yourself.

So in this first part of our journey we have taken a glimpse at death and dying and *The Illusion* of separation that death bestows upon us, what can help and what can hinder. The light of understanding and knowledge allows us to illuminate the dark territory that is our fear. I believe this is really important stuff. It gives us good grounding, just knowing that there is 'something' we can do to help either ourselves or others at a time when chaos seems to be the only order of the day.

But there is just one other thing I would like you to know. It's not part of any grief and bereavement model you will find anywhere, and there are no academic papers to support it, no scientific evidence. It is this: just know that even in our grief there is always a gift somewhere. Sometimes we need to search hard for it. Sometimes it jumps up and hits us over the head. Grief changes us, it changes the way we look at life and death, how we deal with people, and touches us at the very core of our being. We are changed forever. And there is always a gift. In the next part of this book I will bring to you many such 'gifts' that people who are either journeying towards death, or experiencing grief, have received. These gifts often act as a metaphorical smack across the face, propelling us out of *The Illusion* of our loss and into *The Reality* of what *is*.

The gifts themselves are always there, but sometimes we have to be patient as they come unbidden, when we least expect them, and without warning. Sometimes we are so caught up in our pain that we may miss them altogether. These gifts change our lives and our way of being in the world, as anyone who has experienced them will tell you. Once received, the 'gift' cannot be ignored nor forgotten. It becomes a part of our being.

I would like you now to hold on to two concepts.

- Firstly, that it is normal and natural that you maintain a relationship with your loved one who has died. That it continues to grow and flourish albeit in a different way.
- Secondly, we *all* have the ability to do this. Some people do it more readily than others. For some it is just a spontaneous event. Some can turn it on at will. But we all have the innate ability to communicate with someone who has died.

As you hold these two concepts in your mind, let's now take a look at some of the most beautiful experiences that a human being may have in any one lifetime. These experiences are a normal, natural part of the mystery and magic that we have called death, and will inevitably touch all of us at some stage on our own journey. So let's open our souls and our hearts to the magic of *The Reality.*

TRANSITIONS

Throughout life we experience multiple ups and downs, many transitions and losses. Life itself is convoluted and we may undergo mandatory metamorphosis at a moment's notice. As a rule we don't like change, especially if it is accompanied by the pain of loss. But change is inevitable in our lives. Nothing stays the same. Like the tides and the seasons, life is in constant flux.

Each loss we experience throughout life will hold its own unique qualities, flavours and dynamics. Whilst the current loss we are experiencing is often the most painful, grief may open other wounds from our past. Somehow we link it within our minds, store it in the same place as other painful events.

Our smaller losses prepare us for the bigger ones. This is true. It is paradoxical, then, that very little prepares us for our current loss. Nothing could possibly prepare us for this deep sorrow.

Whether we are a support person or whether we are in the midst of our own bereavement, these times can be the most stressful we may experience. In your journal make a list of all the major changes you have under-gone throughout your life. Consider the following:

- What strategies did you employ?

- What *worked* for you?

- How did you get by?

- What strengths did you draw on to help you adapt to the changes?

- What brought you the most comfort?

- What words did you draw strength from?

- In hindsight, what did you learn?

- Often in the learning there is a gift. What gifts did you receive?

- What could you do to bring yourself the most comfort at this point in time?

Part 2

THE REALITY

Dying is like diving into a deep lake on a hot day. There's the shock of that sharp cold change, the pain of it for a second, and then accepting is a swim in reality. But after so many times, even the shock wears off.

Illusions - The Adventures of a Reluctant Messiah

Richard Bach

STORIES

One good thing about being out of the wood is that I can see the stars, the boy said to himself, as the first few stars made themselves visible in the approaching darkness. The shadows of the trees nearby had almost blended in the dusk light. It won't be long now, he thought. Soon it will be dark.

Sure enough, after what seemed like only a short time, darkness was all around him, but he did not feel scared. He had been thinking about the old woman's words. It was true that he loved his parents, and the love that they shared had certainly been a gift. A gift he knew had been torn away from him. The boy also wondered about the old woman's question about looking outside for something that was within. He wondered if she meant within the confines of the wall. He was eager to enter.

At first he did not see the lights, only noises coming from behind the wall. It sounded like people were moving around without talking. Something heavy was being dragged on the ground and every so often he thought he heard a few whispers. More noises, more dragging, then silence again.

I must be dreaming, the boy thought, looking at a flicker of light coming through the entrance. The light is so weak, maybe I am imagining it. But the light grew stronger, and started dancing, creating strange shapes with light and shadow. Should I enter now? The boy was unsure what to do. He did not know what he would find.

The light was becoming stronger and the voices could be heard clearly now. *Who are these people? What will happen to me if I cross the entrance? What will happen to me if I don't?* Unsure of himself, the boy did not feel so brave now. But he heard the old woman's voice inside himself, 'Listen to your heart. It will either tell you to cross, or to walk away. You will know what to do. Trust the voice that talks to you when you are alone.'

Listening intently to that quiet inner voice the boy stood up and, before he could change his mind, shook the soil from his legs and made his way to the entrance. It was like being a small kid again and getting ready to jump in the cold muddy river from the tallest tree; a mixture of fear and excitement. Without hesitating further, he walked over the furrow that the old lady had made, looked up, and froze.

A group of about twenty people sat on animal skins around a large open fire. They were talking to each other in gentle tones. Not one of them turned to look at him.

After standing near the entrance, waiting for a sign of recognition from anyone in the group, the boy slowly advanced. When he was a few feet away from the people, he stopped again. It was pleasant to feel the warmth of the flames on his face, in contrast with the cold air he felt on his back.

Again he waited for someone to acknowledge him. But nobody did. *Are they not talking to me because I do not have a Shadow?* the boy speculated. Unsure what to do, he went to the other side of the group, where a small gap between two people gave him the opportunity to sit near the circle, without really being part of it. And he listened. But he did not understand any of the words. *It must be a foreign language,* he said to himself. *The old woman said I would "understand", but how can I if I don't even speak the same language?* He thought the old woman must be laughing to herself by now, fooling a boy with no Shadow.

The deep sound of a horn interrupted his thoughts. The sound was coming from somewhere in the darkness on the outer edges of the circle. Everybody sat quietly, and the boy did the same.

Just as suddenly as it had started, the sound stopped and a figure stepped forward. *It must be an important person,* the boy thought, *a chief of this tribe.*

The figure came closer to the fire. The boy was so shocked that his mouth fell open, his eyes widened. It was the old woman. Only now she looked younger, taller, in control. She did not even look in the boy's direction.

She seated herself near to the fire, in an empty spot between two men. In her hand she had a small leather bag, a pouch. Her hands fiddled with it as she looked around the circle without resting her gaze on anyone in particular.

As she started talking her voice grew louder so that it could be heard by all. But the boy could not understand a word! He wondered again if this was intentional, so he would not understand. In a circle of many people, the boy with no Shadow suddenly felt very alone.

All faces were transfixed by the woman, everybody intent, listening. After a few more words the lady became quiet, dipped her right hand into the pouch she was holding and grabbed something from within. When her hand came out it was full of black coarse sand. The woman held her hand out in front of her, arm outstretched and said clearly in words that even the boy could understand, 'Our ears listen, but we do not hear. When we hear, we do not understand. We inhale, but we do not breathe. Our heart pulses, but we do not live. We look, but we do not really see. The light blinds us, and darkness frees us.'

The boy was confused; even when he could make sense of the words their meaning escaped him.

At that moment the old woman threw the sand in the fire and a flash of light blinded the boy. His eyelids flickered, but his sight did not return. He was about to get up, feeling scared and confused, when the old woman's voice stopped him.

'Only when you cannot look with your eyes can you see with your soul. Only when you listen with your heart will you understand. Stories will be told, stories that have been lived. Words will be spoken, words that have been heard. Feelings will be shared, feelings that have been felt. Souls will be exposed, souls that have been blessed. In circle we sit, in circle we share. We tell and we learn. As we give of ourselves, the more we become. Let us begin.'

And so it started, one at a time, each looking with their soul, listening with their heart and sharing of themselves. Without being interrupted, each person told his or her tale; tales of life and death, of love and hate, of light and shadow, of right and wrong. They were stories of people, just like him. All searching for something. Each in their way looking for their own Shadow.

The boy, still blind but no longer scared, sat quietly. He listened with his heart, and he heard... all night long...

Five

NEARING-DEATH
AWARENESS

The soul's dark cottage, battered and decayed,
Lets in the new light through chinks that Time has made:
Stronger by weakness, wiser men become
As they draw near to their eternal home.
Leaving the old, both worlds at once they view
That stand upon the threshold of the new.

Old Age

Edmund Waller (Poet – 1608-1666)

The term 'nearing-death awareness' was first introduced by two hospice nurses, Patricia Kelley and Maggie Callanan, in their book *Final Gifts: Understanding the Special Awareness, Needs and Communications of the Dying*. Nearing-death awareness refers to the experience of a very special type of communication by someone who is dying or near death and may include seeing, sensing, speaking to or hearing someone who has already died, or a spiritual being. It also refers to the symbolic language used by someone who is dying which may include planning a trip, or referring to 'going home'. My attention was first brought to nearing-death awareness some years ago when my grandmother died. She announced that Horace, her husband and my grandfather, who had died some years previously, was waiting for her with a bunch of flowers. She died three days later.

Elizabeth Kübler-Ross, in her book entitled *Death Is of Vital Importance – On Life, Death and Life After Death* states, 'There are two kinds of symbolic language (used by the dying): the symbolic nonverbal and the symbolic verbal language. Both are universal languages that you can use all over the world. And once you understand this language, which is the language that children use almost exclusively, then you will never have to guess, you will never have to gamble, and you will begin to understand that **every single dying child, every single dying adult knows – not always consciously, but subconsciously – that they are going to die.**'

But nearing-death awareness is not unique to those who are already dying. Aryan was a fit, healthy nineteen year old, but was well aware that he was going to die before his 20th birthday.

JANINE'S STORY

My son, Aryan, died in a car accident three days before his 20th birthday. It was a bleak and rainy day on November 6th, 2000, and his Commodore came around a bend on the Princes Highway and aqua-planed into the path of a four-wheel drive. He died instantly. We later learned that the bend was a notorious black spot that thankfully has been made safer since my son's death.

Aryan was a real estate agent and his lease-back car was one of the safest on the road. Police reports after the accident confirmed he was not speeding, there were no drugs or alcohol in his system – this was a tragic accident. Somehow though, in the months leading up to it, Aryan knew that it was coming, and did his best to prepare me.

'What do you think happens once we die Mum?' he asked during one of his visits home. It was about two weeks before his accident. He had been touring the coast with a Johnny O'Keefe and Elvis Presley tribute show, and whilst visits home were rare and I missed him, I was so proud of him and how he was living his dream of singing and performing. I stopped what I was doing and replied something like: 'I'm not sure, but I don't believe it's the end of us, I think we continue to live in another form.' It wasn't unusual for us to discuss death and dying, he was always an inquisitive boy and we had had many philosophical discussions over the years.

He then said the words that chilled me to my bone: 'I'm pretty sure I'm going to die young.'

We were sitting on the veranda, overlooking the ocean. I looked at him but he was staring off into the distance, lost in his own thoughts. My heart was pounding so fast it hurt and I wanted so badly to dismiss what he said as fantasy – he was young and healthy and had his whole life ahead of him. The problem was, he had touched upon a fear within me that I had harboured his whole life – a fear that had evolved into full crippling panic attacks over the preceding months – that I was going to lose this precious child and there was nothing I could do about it. I found the strength to remain calm and let him talk: 'Are you mate? Do you know how you are going to die?' I asked.

'I think it's a car accident.'

I don't remember much of what was said after that. I probably gave him the third degree about the safety of his tyres. But I am so grateful that I was able to allow him to share this burden with me. I am his mother, I gave him his life, and for a brief moment, he gave me a glimpse into his death. What a terrible but precious moment.

After Aryan's funeral, my husband, Eric (Aryan's stepfather), confided in me that, on that same visit home, Aryan had asked to speak with him. Aryan asked Eric to promise him that he would look after his mum, and when Eric had replied, 'Of course I will mate, you know that.' Aryan made him shake hands on it. Eric didn't understand why Aryan was so insistent, but took it seriously and gave him his promise, and is glad that he did.

Looking back over Aryan's life, I realise that he always suspected he was going to die young. He would often tell me that he couldn't imagine himself any older than 20. He told me several times, over the years, that he would never be married, never have children. He didn't dramatise it, just stated it as fact. I often wonder: why was he so sure about these things, how could he possibly know? Was it a blessing that he was aware of what was to come, or did this knowledge scare him? On a dark day I am haunted by the feeling that he struggled alone with his premonitions. On a good day, when my grief has ebbed and mortality makes some sort of sense to me, I believe his knowledge was a gift that enabled him to live life more fully than most young men his age.

And then there were my own premonitions, my own terrors of losing him. A month before he died I dreamt that the town was flooded, and my girls were on dry land but no-one could find Aryan. In my dream I swam like I had never swum before, calling for him, diving under the water and searching frantically for him through the debris. I woke up gasping for air, and was soon comforted by the knowledge that it was only a dream.

The day before he died he was meant to meet me at Darling Harbour for lunch but, in typical Aryan fashion, he forgot. It didn't matter, I was with friends anyhow, and I knew I would hear from him soon enough, full of apologies.

The call came that night. 'Mum I'm so sorry! I've got so much going on at the moment! Do you forgive me?'

As if I wouldn't! 'Well, I suppose so,' I said. 'You're lucky I love you so much.'

'You're beautiful Mama,' he said to me. I remember feeling so much love for him at that moment that, inexplicably, it brought me to tears.

I said something like, 'Well you have to say it twice, seeing as you made me wait.'

And he said, 'You're beautiful, beautiful Mama.' These were the last words we ever spoke to each other, and what comfort they bring to me. I believe this is the gift of nearing-death awareness — the opportunity to share how we feel about each other, the chance to say our goodbyes. And how can I ever question the reality of life beyond death, when there is so much we don't understand.

When Aryan was growing up he was often sick from asthma, and at times would be quite delirious with fever. I would sit up with him while he tossed and turned and mumbled in his sleep. One night he sat up and said, 'Mum, the man with white hair is there, he's waiting for me. I'm scared.'

I had a cold flannel on his forehead and I soothed him: 'Shhh, it's OK. Tell the man with white hair to go away, you're not going with him.' My son soon settled down, but over the years, I often wondered about this particular delirium.

One month after my son's death I went to see a clairvoyant. She told me Aryan was with us and he was safe. She said, 'He said to tell you the man with white hair was there to greet him.'

One cannot help but be moved by Janine's experience; it is most profound.

More often the awareness of death is subconscious, and the use of symbolic language may be subtle, but detectable nonetheless, if we really listen. I remember well my uncle Donald just before he died, at the end of his last conversation with my dad said formally, 'Goodbye Kenneth.' My dad commented at the time that this was strange as they never said 'goodbye' to each other, it was always 'see you later' or some such, never goodbye. Neither did his brother call him 'Kenneth', it was always 'Ken'. Uncle Donald died only a week after that goodbye. This is a typical example of the symbolic language used by the dying. And it happens time and time again. Uncle Donald instinctively knew he would not talk with my dad again. It was a formal farewell. It still makes me tear up that the card sent with the flowers to the funeral from us simply said, 'Goodbye Donald' in response.

Sometimes the nearing-death awareness is somehow 'tuned into' by a close family member. Janine was also experiencing an 'awareness' of her son's impending death. This often happens when two people are closely in sync with each other.

In this next story, Francesca 'knows', albeit unconsciously, that her father is about to die, and so says the very thing that needs to be said at just the right moment.

Francesca's Story

My father loved gardening. He loved me too. We were fortunate to share some very special time before his unexpected death; time that has given me great comfort in the years that have since passed; time that has helped me to understand that when a loved one passes, all is in its place; the universe has a master plan, and everything is just as it should be.

When my partner and I bought our first home, my father was delighted for us. He could be heard bragging to friends and neighbours about our success, and proudly announcing that I had found my 'dream home'. It was true, the house was just what I had wanted but, even better, the gardens were ready-made. Although I loved plants, I had never been much of a gardener, so an added attraction of my new home was the bonus of all my favourite plants readily established. All I had to do was maintain it.

My father's first visit became an exciting adventure of discovery through a magical flora. We wandered amongst shrubs and ferneries, groundcover leaching scents beneath our steps. My father shared his expert knowledge regarding the plants' species, and offered helpful tips for care and maintenance. Sharing a love for camellia flowers, my father and I agreed that it would be a wonderful surprise in the following months to learn the colours of the three camellia trees. He explained that although he could attest to the difference between their species (japonica and sasanqua), he could not predict the colour of their blooms. It was like having my own personal nursery assistant! But even better, I revelled in the knowledge that this garden was truly magical; it offered a space for my father and I to share precious time together. I loved my father dearly, yet had found that the natural progression of my life beyond early adolescence had distanced me from his company. Now was an exciting and wonderful opportunity for us to reconnect, and continue to share in the joy that had always characterised our relationship when we were young.

I had always known my father loved me. As a young child, when friends bragged that they had the best dad in the world, I would respond in kind, 'No, I have the best dad in the world.' Only secretly, I knew I really did! There was nothing my father would not do for me. He never raised his voice, but I always knew when I had disappointed him, and that was worse than any shouting or punishment. My dad was the most friendly, generous, understanding, selfless person, who always had time for games, help with problems, and letting me be myself. And to top it off, I was adopted, so I knew I was wanted and loved.

The funny thing was, 'love' was never mentioned in our family. It was an unspoken code, something we shared and actioned, but never verbally mentioned. Now, in my adult life, I understand that my parents' own upbringings, the stiff upper-lipped Anglo version, did not engender verbal gushings of endearment, and so my parents simply carried on the way they knew. As a child, there was never a lack of love in my home; we just never said, 'I love you'.

Two weeks after my father's first visit to my new home, I telephoned my parents. It was Mother's Day. My father answered the phone and I soon found myself deep in discussion of plans for his next visit, when he was to bring his gardening gear and together we would pursue some horticultural activity. In actuality, nothing really needed to be done; we just enjoyed the idea of sharing time together. The only thing to be achieved in my garden was the discovery of the colour of the camellia flowers and, to this end, my father and I deliberated endlessly, making bets and sharing visions. Remembering it was

Mother's Day, I asked my father to put my mother on the phone. As I said farewell to my father, something totally unexpected occurred. As if possessed by an external force, the words, 'I love you Dad,' erupted from my being. Before I could reconcile what had happened the silence of shock had passed, and my father had left to fetch my mother.

Later that day the phone rang, and it was my dad. He made some insignificant small talk, before saying goodbye and then announcing, 'By the way, I love you too!'

That was the last time I spoke with my dad.

The next weekend I answered the phone to my very shaken mother, who gently informed me that my father had been rushed to hospital. Having suffered a massive stroke, he was unconscious and on life support. The neurosurgeon informed us there was nothing that could be done. Our only comfort was in knowing that Dad felt nothing, and that the severity of his stroke meant that he did not have to endure a debilitated existence — a fear he had strongly expressed in the past. Our only course of action was to consent to the removal of life support and await the inevitable.

And that was where the magic began.

We sat speechless, my brother, my mother and I. The hospital room's austerity spoke nothing of the love and joy that had characterised our family's past. Yet ironically, the starkness commanded that something be said between my brother and me. You see, because of extended family disagreements, my brother and I had not talked to each other for years. This had pained my father deeply, and he had tried every possible avenue to help us reconcile our differences and bring our family back together. So here we sat, sharing the same fears, sharing the same Anglo-upbringing, equally unable to express how very scared and saddened we were, both at the loss of our dad, and at our inability to be loving in his final hour.

Dad was transferred from the ICU to a ward, and we sat with him as the machinery was removed, and his brain somehow willed him to breathe independently. For hours, we waited with Dad, each of us pacing the hospital halls in turn. On a tea run to the vending machine, I met my brother in the hall. We both faced each other, leaning casually against opposite walls. I cannot recall who spoke first; it is insignificant now anyway. I discovered that we both shared the desire for Dad to make a miraculous recovery, as well as the knowledge that no matter how much we willed it, Dad was no longer with us and we had to say goodbye. And as if possessed once again, an involuntary utterance escaped me. 'I love you Pete,' sprang forth from my mouth, before I could catch it back along with my pride. My brother and I embraced, nothing more was spoken, but we understood each other's love for each other and acceptance of the way life had unfolded.

My father stopped breathing within the next hour. I have said ever since, he had waited for my brother and I to reconcile, and had died peacefully in the knowledge that we would be okay.

That was just after midnight on Saturday night. I spent an empty and lonely Sunday with my mother, before returning home to my family Sunday evening. The next morning I awoke and sat in the late autumn chill, staring from my window at my beautiful garden that I had shared so briefly, but so wholesomely with my dad. And seeing the camellia tree, my breath escaped me. A wash of joy flooded every cell of my body as I caught sight of the miracle before my eyes. Delicate and vulnerable, solitary and proud, as uplifting as heaven itself, the first bloom of the season announced itself to the world, 'I am here. I am soft pink. I am.'

Every aspect of the flower's existence resonated with the legacy of my father. I knew, as sure as any wisdom that resides in the depths of the heart, that flower was sent by an angel that was now my dad.

And so it was that the camellia tree took a further three weeks to put forth many more blooms. And as I watched the development of my father's flower, open abundantly, live richly and fully, before gradually wilting and fading with the passing of time, I knew, as sure as any wisdom that resides in the depths of the heart, that everything in this world is in its place, and is just as it is meant to be.

For Francesca and her dad the timing and the synchronicity, woven throughout those last few weeks of precious moments together, beautifully illustrates the sheer perfection of the order of events, the planning of which could not have been more elegant.

In this next story David actually sees his wife appear to him before she dies. It is as though her spirit is already starting to move outside her body before death has taken place. These moments are most special, as David well knows.

David's Story

My wife, Dee, had been in palliative care for a number of weeks and was in a coma and dying of breast cancer. I had thrown myself into my work and, when I wasn't visiting her, I was seeing clients at all hours.

It was a Saturday. I had finished working and had made myself a sandwich and a cuppa for lunch. Having eaten, I was resting and thinking of leaving to visit Dee. Suddenly, there she was in front of me. She looked at me and said, 'It will soon be time for me to leave.' Her image and voice were crystal clear and I knew that, at last, she was prepared to leave our two daughters and me. I said to her, 'I'm so pleased you are ready to go. I'll be fine, and so will our daughters.' As soon as I said this, the image disappeared.

I phoned the hospice immediately to speak to my eldest daughter who had been with Dee throughout the morning. I asked her, 'How's Mum?' She said, 'She is behaving most strangely. Her eyes have opened and she is trying to tell me something.' I said, 'I know what she wants to tell you. We haven't got long, she is going to leave us soon. I will soon be there.'

A friend of ours phoned and said that he and his wife would like to see Dee. I said that I would meet them at the hospice, however, they might not be able to see her, as there wasn't much time left.

When I arrived at the hospice my other daughter was there, having travelled down from the Blue Mountains. Our friends arrived shortly after with a bunch of yellow roses, which happened to be Dee's favourite flower and colour. I couldn't let them see Dee as she was very close to death.

My daughters and I sat around her bedside and I put both my arms across her to give her Reiki energy, and told her when she was ready, she could leave us, safe in the knowledge that we would be okay. Within five minutes she had peacefully died and my daughters and I were so pleased that any pain and suffering was over and she had left quietly.

David sadly passed away in late 2011, before this book was published and I'd just like to say, *Cheerio David, our chat about your story is very well cherished and remembered.*

As in David's story above, nearing-death awareness can bring comfort, give warning and prepare us for what is about to happen. Sometimes it can be scary, even if we do have a basic belief in consciousness surviving bodily death.

This next story illustrates the power of nearing-death awareness to bring about comfort for the person who is dying. This story is also about after-death communication but I believe needs to be told in its entirety, so I include it here as such.

KERRY'S STORY

My husband, Wal, died from motor neurone disease, which is a disease in which every muscle of the body dies, sometimes quite fast, sometimes quite slowly. In Wal's case it was quite fast. He was diagnosed in April and died in November.

But it was the day prior to his death that was quite calming for him. I went into our bedroom where Wal was resting and he said to me, 'I've just had a visitor.'

At this time, we lived on a farm 25 kilometres from nowhere, so I knew that nobody had come into the house. But Wal was quite awake and quite lucid, so had not been dreaming. He took no drugs whatsoever, only aspirin for pain control.

Wal told me, 'This fellow was dressed in a checked shirt and corduroy pants. I don't know him, I haven't seen him before. As he came through the doorway he said to me, "How are you going mate?" And I said to him, "Okay." He looked at me and he said, "I want to talk to you but I'll come back tomorrow," and with that he walked across the room and straight through the wall.'

My husband died the next day.

While this was comforting for Wal, I'm afraid, on the day of his death, it was of no real comfort to me. The grief was just overwhelming and I took no comfort in anything. And although I had quite a strong faith and although the death was probably about six weeks earlier than expected and quite sudden, I thought I'd be prepared, but I was not. I'm not sure if anything really prepares you for that moment. So the appearance of the gentleman who visited my husband was of no great solace to me. And it didn't change any aspect of my grief.

It was to be over a year before Kerry's time would come for her to experience her own communication that was to affect her profoundly and bring unexpected comfort to her bereavement. Kerry goes on to tell us;

What did in fact have a great bearing on the grief that I was carrying came probably about 18 months later, when I was with a practitioner who was doing some bodywork. I'd had a dreadful time dealing with various aspects of the estate and other issues and I was finding it difficult to cope. I was having some bodywork and I was relaxed, but certainly not in any other state except relaxed. I'd been chatting a little earlier to the girl who was doing the bodywork and then I was just quiet. And what happened next did have a profound effect on my grief and quietened my fears, hurt, anguish and loneliness.

My husband actually spoke to me. It was not that the practitioner could hear; it was in my head. It was most definitely Wal's voice. There was no doubt in my mind about that. And he spoke to me on a subject that I would not have thought that he would speak of should there be any communication between us.

He actually spoke about our wedding vows, what they had meant to him, how much I meant to him, the fact that he would go on believing that those vows would last forever. It was quite some minutes that he was speaking. I was shocked. Shocked and surprised. When the girl who was doing the bodywork started to say something I had to signal her to stop so that I could listen more intently.

Unfortunately I did not have pen and paper with me, nor could I ask for them for fear of interrupting. So I had forgotten some of the exact words that were said, but they were very soothing and they were very reassuring. I suppose in many ways it gave me a faith back in life after death. It lifted my spirits greatly and it gave me a great sense of relief to know Wal was okay. I believe there is a greater power and somewhere out there is my husband. I only hope that sometime, in the years ahead, I can hear that wonderful voice again.

Nearing-death awareness often occurs during the 24 to 36 hours prior to death, but may also spontaneously occur at other times when our life may be threatened or in danger. Nearing-death awareness may also occur, as in the case with my dad, if we are moving towards the journey we call death and can happen many months before actual death.

This next story is just extraordinary. Here is Kathi's beautiful story.

KATHI'S STORY

My grandmother, Marie Fletcher, who died a few years ago, told me that when she was a young woman her brother, Ashley, was a soldier fighting at Gallipoli. At the time, my gran was nursing her own grandmother who was old, sick and nearing death. Just before the old woman died, her face lit up and she smiled and said, 'Ashley! What are you doing here?' And then she died. News soon came that Ashley had been killed at Gallipoli just before his grandmother passed away. My gran always believed that Ashley's spirit had come to greet his grandmother's spirit at the moment of her death, so soon after his own.

In his book, *Palliative Care Perspectives*, Dr J L Hallenbeck states, 'In normal wakefulness, we function and interact on a relatively narrow and shared frequency that allows both transmission and reception of shared experiences. When patients at the end of life experience altered states, it is as if their radio frequency, their wavelength, has shifted.' He goes on to say, '(This) allows the patient to experience both the "normal" wavelength on which we coexist and yet receive signals on a wavelength that we cannot perceive. Such a patient might be perfectly aware of being in a hospital bed and of dying but be able to see and hear a deceased relative sitting in a chair next to the bed.' An interesting analogy.

Here's a lovely story from Pauline about what happened in the hours before her father's death. He appears to be able to see and communicate with something that only he was 'privileged to see'. This is reflective of Dr Hallenbeck's statement above.

PAULINE'S STORY

Grief was not an unknown emotion to me. My father was the second youngest of ten children and there always seemed to be a funeral in the family. As children, my sister and I frequently played at the cemetery, adorning graves with flowers and twig arrangements. I felt that I was equipped with a sound understanding of grief which would enable me to handle the inevitable death of my parents. Yet, close to the time of my father's death, I was to witness something which would enable me to experience grief in a more tangible way than I had imagined.

My father had battled with the complications of bowel cancer and by the end of his eighty-fourth year our family was caring for him in his home on a rotational basis. The night before he died, I cared for my father and as he lay gravely ill on the bed next to me, I watched in awe as he raised his shrunken, feeble body to an upright position, arms outstretched to heaven and softly called the names of his deceased brothers and sisters. I moved closer to hear his voice in anticipation of seeing what he could see, but only he was privileged to see his siblings. He named them: Eily, Elsie, Molly, Eddie...

As he slowly returned to his comatose position, I retreated to my bed, weeping with mixed emotions, for I knew his siblings' call was strong and that my father's death was imminent. Early the next morning, the doctor arranged for my father to be moved into palliative care. Once he was settled in I prepared to return home to freshen up. However, the sister in charge advised I gather my family and stay as my father was extremely close to passing away. This occurred in a peaceful, serene manner. I felt calm and reassured that everything was as it should be.

The next few days were filled with emotion, but I knew where my father was, who he was with and the joy he would have been experiencing. Oh, the yarns and stories the O'Keefe siblings would have been sharing! How fortunate I was to have an insight into his journey after death and how much easier it has been for me to manage grief since that experience.

I believe what is happening is that as we move nearer to death our brain patterns, our frequency of vibration changes which makes it easier to see other things that are out of our normal range of sensory perception.

There are animals, of course, which, as a normal part of their nature, are able to see or hear or perceive on a wider range than humans. The humble dog has a far greater range of hearing than we do, and so is able to hear what we cannot. We take this for granted. There are some forms of fish that follow magnetic patterns in the earth's energy field over thousands of miles. It has been suggested that many other species such as whales, bees and even pigeons also use these lines of energy. They have inbuilt sensors that can detect the energy fields. Snakes have special organs that allow them to perceive in the ultraviolet range, and so sense heat from their prey. Dolphins use sonar to perceive objects, but do not sense a solid object as we would imagine. Rather they pick up shapes and the movement of internal organs which can be compared to the images seen on an ultrasound scan. Their reality is difficult for us to comprehend. **Science does not know the full range of sensory abilities possible.** The phenomena surrounding nearing-death awareness and the tuning into other ways of sensing are a primary example of this.

So, some species have the ability to detect things that we cannot sense. Rupert Sheldrake, a prominent scientist and author, has conducted many studies on dogs, cats and even a parrot, all of whom sense when a particular family member is about to phone home, but are unconcerned when other people call. In one case a cat knew when its 'mother' was going to phone home and he would sit on the phone seat and purr. When the owner went overseas on a trip the cat went to the phone at 1 am in the morning and its 'father' saw the cat and told it that it was useless sitting there purring because 'she's not ringing at this time'. But sure enough this lady did ring a few seconds later, out of the blue. This is not an uncommon phenomenon.

I have a dear friend who told me about an amazing experience with her daughter's black cocker spaniel, who literally saved a life.

Lyn's Story

It was night time and my daughter and son-in-law were watching TV. The five-month-old baby was tucked into his cot, fast asleep - a precious son, a much wanted child.

Oscar, the jet black cocker spaniel was in the sitting room, happily dozing, when suddenly, he got up, very alert, and went to the door leading into the baby's room.

He whimpered and scratched at the door. My daughter, curious to know what he was doing, opened the door to the child's room.

Oscar went straight to the cot, put his forelegs on the side of the cot and whimpered more insistently.

My daughter went to the sleeping child, listened for his breathing, couldn't hear it. She put her hand close to his nose in order to feel his breath and, again, couldn't feel it.

She called for her husband to come and lifted the child up...and he started to breathe.

Was this a case of Oscar sensing something outside of human range? Who knows. I like to believe that he saved my grandson's life and I know that I am eternally grateful.

Indeed there are some dogs that can sense when their owner is going to have a seizure, often quite some time before it happens. They are trained to do it. The dog is tuning into a change in brain frequencies.

The point I am making is that it is possible to tune into other frequencies, hearing, seeing, sensing, that we don't normally experience. We as humans only perceive a small window of what is possible and this is limited to our sensory organs.

Some people are also attuned to other 'frequencies'. Let's meet Maureen...

MAUREEN'S STORY

My earliest 'awarenesses' as a child were always squashed - usually I was sent to bed and pronounced 'over-excited' or 'over-imaginative'! Needless to say, I do not remember the exact reasons for the banishments.

However, about 15 to 20 years ago I was standing with a close friend in her kitchen when, what I now call "THE VOICE" said, 'You have breast cancer.' This was an internal voice which I kept to myself. However, my concern was sufficient that I made sure my friend did have her yearly breast check which was due, and yes, she did have breast cancer. She survived for 10 or more years but one day she and I were again standing in her kitchen and THE VOICE said, 'Your head is very dark.' This did not make much sense to me but shortly afterwards she was diagnosed with secondaries in the bones in her skull (which showed up as dark areas on the x-rays). She died about a year later.

And again, as her husband and I sat in the waiting room at Calvary Hospital one day, I was told that, 'It will not be long now.' My friend died that evening.

THE VOICE in all these health and death instances was very CLEAR AND STRONG.

These pieces of information I had received I found disturbing until I discovered Dr Caroline Myss's work in her first book, Anatomy of the Spirit, *and read about her work as a Medical Intuitive with Dr Norman Shealy.*

I became aware that in the past I had had many such Voice Visitations - always dismissed as my imagination (and of course bad).

After my experience with my friend with breast cancer, I took greater heed and when I told a woman I worked with that she would have an easy birth - it just slipped out of my mouth. And she did - her first baby in 3 hours - I realised that perhaps this was not just about death. At the time I was very embarrassed by my involuntary statement.

Clairaudience for me is often very difficult to distinguish from the monkey mind chatter - except when the Voice is very strong as in the birth and illness situations.

I had a friend who was custodian of a large area of sacred Aboriginal Land in the Blue Mountains. He had been diagnosed with multiple myeloma but treatments were ceasing to be effective and he was, I thought, in Tasmania with his daughter. I was driving from Mudgee to Sydney and, as I came to the turn off to the Bells Line of Road at Mount Victoria, I had instruction to go to "the name of the land" where my friend was, and that he required a lift back to Sydney. I nearly did not go, again dismissing it as nonsense. At the last minute I turned left and, when I arrived at the property, my friend was there, his backpack on, ready to take the train to Sydney. He did not seem surprised to see me. That was the last time I saw him as he died shortly afterwards.

So generally THE VOICE is at its most insistent and strongest when the information concerns sickness or death.

I understand that one can train in 'Medical Intuitiveness' but I have never taken that step.

I am very interested to know what is it about disease and dying that triggers the clairaudient reaction. I think perhaps in my case the early suppression of this ability only allows in those pieces of information that are relevant to dying.

GOD'S PAINT

Take a break. Go outside and find a flower in your garden. If you don't have a garden you might like to go and buy yourself a small bunch of flowers. Find one flower that you are particularly drawn to. Spend a few moments really looking at this flower. Notice its perfection, the depth of colour – whether it is a subtle shade or vibrant and deep, the symmetry, the texture of the petals. Be absorbed by its beauty. Just for a moment, turn yourself over to the contemplation of this flower. Listen to its language, its whisperings.

Allow your awareness to linger in its beauty, its perfection. It has been said that flowers are God's paint. Now ask yourself this, if God could create something so beautiful, so magnificent, so perfect, as this flower how could anything be other than perfect? It may not be as we would like it to be, but it is still perfect. Trust that there is nothing but divine order in life and in death. Something so beautiful, so perfect could not be created by something that was not perfect in itself. Trust in divine order.

Take out your journal and pen and consider the following:

- What feelings arise from this exercise?

- What thoughts flow through your mind as you contemplate the perfection that is this flower?

- What wisdom does this flower whisper?

- Record anything else that you feel is relevant.

Six

NEAR-DEATH EXPERIENCE

'Oh, Fletch, come on. Think. If you are talking to me now, then obviously you didn't die, did you? What you did manage to do was to change your level of consciousness rather abruptly.'

Jonathan Livingston Seagull

Richard Bach

T he near-death experience presents yet another piece of the fascinating puzzle of life and death. According to studies outlined by the International Association of Near-Death Studies Inc., near-death experiences are phenomena that occur in approximately 4% to 15% of the population. Many people say that they felt feelings of peacefulness, love and acceptance at the time of the near-death experience. A small percentage of people report that this was a frightening and unpleasant experience, one they would not wish to repeat.

Since the groundbreaking work of Dr Raymond Moody, who was the first to bring these experiences out of the closet and to the fore in his book *Life after Life*, there has been much interest and subsequent research conducted in various parts of the world.

More recently the work of Dr Sam Parnia, a medical doctor from the UK, has caught the attention of many. He is founder of the Horizon Research Foundation, and is the UK's leading expert on near-death experiences. In his book, *What Happens When We Die*, Dr Parnia discusses his work with patients who have had cardiac arrest and have subsequently 'flat lined'. He hypothesises that it would be impossible for the brain to be capable of ordered thought or to lay down any memories whatsoever at the point of 'flat line' as there is no electrical activity in the brain. However, it would appear that this is exactly what happens in some people.

It is important to understand that no two near-death experiences are alike. Each one is like a fingerprint, as unique and individual as the person who is having the experience. One thing that these experiences seem to have in common, almost without exception, is that they are very real and life changing events.

Near-death experiences are characterised by the following:

OUT-OF-BODY EXPERIENCE

Often one of the first things people who have had a near-death experience notice is that they move outside their body. This has been called the out-of-body experience. People who have near-death experiences often report being able to view from above what is happening to them and can see doctors working on them. Many can recall quite accurate details of medical procedures, what the doctor has said etc. A common feeling is of floating above one's own body and looking down on what is happening.

Out-of-body experiences may also happen independently of being close to death. There are many accounts of people having out-of-body experiences who are just traumatised by an event, but who are not close to dying. Still more puzzling, some people have out-of-body experiences when they are not in any danger whatsoever. Children are particularly susceptible to out-of-body experiences during dreaming.

KATHI'S STORY

My son, Jack, has always had very vivid and often terrifying dreams. Many times he has dreamt of deadly situations in which he gets badly injured but narrowly survives. When he was ten years old, he dreamt that he was set on fire, and the burning was so ferocious that, in his dream, he actually died. At the point of his own death, he could feel his spirit start to leave his body. As this happened, he woke up and continued to feel his spirit move out of his body. On realising what was happening, he became terrified, and instantly his spirit pulled back inside him. He believes that if his spirit hadn't pulled back inside, he would have died that night. He also believes that what he dreamt was what it must really be like for a person at the point of death, when the spirit gently starts to leave the body.

BARBARA'S STORY

I took my six-year-old son on a trip to the snow, catching a plane from Sydney to Canberra, and then a coach which would eventually take us to the snow fields. When we arrived, at around 9pm, the restaurant at the motel was closed, so we went for a walk to find a shop so we could buy something to eat. It was a freezing cold night and after arriving back at the motel we found it necessary to put towels up against the door to stop the draft coming into our room. My son in one bed and myself in the other, we both went to sleep. I awoke to find myself floating on the ceiling of the room. I could see my son asleep in his bed and my bed looked slept in. All I could think was 'I do not want my son to be alone, he is only six years old.' I fought and fought to get back to the bed and finally I got back and went back to sleep. Our trip continued the next day as planned. This happened over 30 years ago and I have never forgotten it.

INTENSE FEELINGS

Feelings of love, peace and wellbeing may arise during the near-death experience; often these feelings are so intense there is a physical quality to them. Many people find it hard to describe the intensity of the feelings that permeate their being. Often people feel more alive and more vibrant than they ever have before.

MOVING THROUGH A TUNNEL

Many people experience movement through a dark tunnel towards an intense bright light, followed by the perception of emerging from this tunnel into another place, often either a spiritual place or garden. It is here that there may be a rapid review of life events, the details of which seem to flash past in a split second. People often report that bad events, the things they feel they did wrong during their life will also appear here, but there is no judgement. They simply watch them pass without attachment. The impact of their actions may also be shown, but again this is without judgment. It just simply 'is'.

GREETED BY A DECEASED RELATIVE OR SPIRITUAL BEING

Often the person is greeted either by dead relatives or a spiritual being. Some people report that they cannot 'see' anyone, but feel or sense a presence. This being or presence is often reported as being wise, all-loving, all-forgiving, all-knowing.

A Return to Body

People who have a near-death experience are told to return at some point and find themselves back in their body, experiencing the pain of the trauma to their bodies. Some say they feel as though they are being drawn back down the tunnel in order to return. Many feel disappointed or cheated by this as they want to regain the intense feelings of love, peace and acceptance that the near-death experience brings.

All of these are characteristic of the classic near-death experience. A person who has a near-death experience might encounter all or only a few of these events.

Here is an unusual near-death experience that gives me goose bumps. It really does offer a glimpse into the fascinating experience of death.

Lyn's Story

My uncle, who lived many kilometres away, was undergoing an operation during which he almost died. It was later that my uncle told me that, during the operation, he saw his deceased mother standing at the gate of their family home. He knew she was calling out something and moved closer so he could hear.

When he reached her she told him, 'I don't want you, I want your brother.'

What is odd is that my father suffered a heart attack and died whilst his brother's operation was in progress. My uncle witnessed their mother calling his brother home.

This is a particularly interesting account as Lyn's uncle could not possibly be aware that his brother had died, since he was in theatre at the time.

When Greg was just 15 years old he was suffering from an asthma attack and went into a coma, and although this happened many years ago it is still very vividly remembered.

GREG'S STORY

It was a Friday in April or May, 1972, that my mother took me to have a medical check up at the clinic some kilometres away from home. Because of the distance involved, I had made arrangements to stay at my mate's place for the weekend.

My mother was going to leave all my tablets, but she had left without doing so, so all I had was Alupent spray to help me breathe. During the night I was not feeling too well, so I just kept puffing on the spray. By morning I had taken too much and woke up in a sweat. My mate decided to call an ambulance. However, because he was only fifteen years old, the person receiving the call thought it was a hoax, and refused to send one out. He then rang for a taxi to take me to hospital.

The taxi arrived and I noticed it was a white HR Holden with a red interior. That's when I went into what I believe was a coma. The next thing I remember was the doctors working on me and I was hovering above myself. Then I noticed a bright light shining down a tunnel and suddenly I was in the tunnel. I saw a hand waving me back. I looked down at myself lying very still and I noticed my mum and my sister crying. The next thing I remembered was waking up the following Tuesday or Wednesday. I said to the doctor, 'I died, didn't I?' He replied, 'Yes, but you're here now.'

*I am now 52 years old and it has made me unafraid of dying. Dying happens to us all. It was just **not** my turn then.*

One thing that seems to dominate these stories is that it is life changing. It changes the way in which people view life and death.

Most report not being afraid of dying, of feeling more in touch with their spirituality, becoming much more in tune with their environment, their family and friends. Things that seemed important to them are no longer so. They begin to realise the things that are important are relationships and love, and material things become less of an attraction.

When I was conducting research in preparation for this book, a fellow contacted me to tell me of a friend who had one such near-death experience. He had been a 'bit of a rebel', always in some sort of trouble and had many brushes with the law. After having a near-death experience he did a complete turnaround, got involved with his local church, started doing voluntary work and became a really caring person.

In short these experiences produce profound change. I believe it is for this reason that near-death experiences are so interesting. The changes that take place seem to be permanent. They last. This is another reason why these experiences are so important. The therapeutic application of the near-death experience for people who are suffering depression or perhaps who have maladapted behaviours would seem to merit exploration. We will look at this a little later on.

Jacqueline's story begins with a visit to her local family doctor.

JACQUELINE'S STORY

It was in August, 2007, that I finally decided to go to the family doctor. I'd had a bit of chest pain, not severe, but I'd been putting off going for months. I was a naughty girl because I had already had a couple of mild heart attacks. Anyway, off I went and saw him and he said, 'First off, we're going to do an x-ray.' So I popped in next door and had an x-ray. Then he said, 'Now pop into the next room and have your ECG done and then we'll have a talk about it.' So I did. After the nurse did the ECG she asked me if I had any pain now. I told her that I still had a bit of pain. And she came straight over and asked me to open my mouth, so I did, obligingly, and she sprayed nitrate spray under my tongue. And I was quite happily sitting on the side of the bed. She went back over to the other side of the room and she said to me, 'You might like to lie down, because some people feel a bit funny after they have this spray.' I said, 'No, I'm fine.' The next minute my words to her were, 'I feel dreadful, I feel dreadful.' I don't remember but I must have laid myself back. I could hear her clearly scream out to the doctor, 'Come now, come now.' This must have been on the telephone. He came in and I was still there, but I could feel myself going and I knew I couldn't do anything about it. I didn't try to fight it; it was almost like I didn't want to. It was just the same as if I was going under anaesthetic.

So the doctor had my left hand and he was hitting it constantly. I was just fading and thinking to myself, 'This is going to be lovely when this pain goes. If only this awful feeling would go I'd feel a whole lot better.' I didn't think about whether I was going to die or anything. I just thought maybe I was going to faint or go to sleep. I can still feel the doctor hitting the back of my hand. I can hear his last words to me, which were, 'Jacky, I'm going to get Harold.'

Now I think this is probably where I departed. I don't remember. My husband told me later that when he came in, the doctor said it was very serious. Harold came in, he held my hand and told me, 'It's alright darling, I'm here now.' But I didn't hear any of that. All I knew was that suddenly I felt in a nice place. I felt good. I'm very, very claustrophobic, but I didn't feel claustrophobic at all. I was breathing stronger than I've ever breathed before. And I felt really, really good. But funnily enough, I could only sense from my head down to my waist. I just didn't have any feeling or thought of legs or anything. I was lying there quite peacefully in my own little world.

And then quite suddenly this most absurd thought came into my brain. It was on the left-hand side, almost to the left of me, not on a screen, but there it was...Names, not so much images of people, but only the names of my family came very, very fast. It was given to me very quickly. Firstly my daughter, Kylie, then Chris, and Hayley. Then my son, Grant. Then Megan, Taylor and Harold. My poor husband is still getting over the fact that he was last and not first.

But they were given to me so quickly and next the wording, 'They'll be alright.' Then I thought to myself, 'What in the hell am I thinking about this now for? What in the hell's this all about?' Then the next minute I get this thought given to me or I'm sort of saying out aloud, 'I thought someone's supposed to meet me.' And that was the end of it. I thought to myself, 'Why on earth would I think that?' I didn't think anything before then; it just came into my mind.

The next thing I knew the doctor's leaning over saying to me, 'Jacky, you have to go to hospital.' I'm aware that now there are two ambulance men that are in the room there, fussing over me, preparing me. I am aware that my husband is there, but I don't take any notice of him.

I don't know at what stage I died. As far as I was concerned I was alive and kicking, so maybe I was just waiting for somebody to come and meet me and when that didn't happen it got taken out from underneath me. And I didn't know this of course; I didn't know how I came back...I didn't think I'd even gone really; I didn't know I was dead. But I know now that the only reason I was brought back was because the ambulance men were driving past the doctor's surgery when the call went through and they pulled in along the street and it was the paddles that brought me back. Otherwise I would have still been floating up there and speaking with Mum and Dad and everybody else.

They discharged me four days later, satisfied that I was going to live. When I had the next angiogram, it proved to be good. My heart was okay.

One thing I do feel. I should have had counselling. I believe all of us should have counselling, even if it's only a group therapy session, to get together and exchange experiences. But looking back on that week or two, and for many, many months after that, I was very, very cross.

About a week or so later I was telling a friend about what had happened. I said to her during the conversation that I felt a little bit aggro about it. I said, 'Nothing's changed.'

She said, 'What do you mean, nothing's changed?'

I said, 'Nothing's changed. Everything's the same. I've kind of been and seen enough down here and it's very nice and everything, but it's boring. It's nothing different.'

So she said to me, 'Well, what did you expect!'

'It's so mundane, I've still got to iron and cook and all the rest of it.'

She said, 'So!' And we laughed. I think talking with my friend helped me a bit.

I went back to see my doctor and I thanked him for what he had done. I asked him if he had prayed for me and he said he had. Then I said to him, 'But since then, I've changed, I'm terribly outspoken now. And I don't like the way I've just suddenly become. I'm not thinking anymore, not holding everything to myself. I'm speaking it out now. I'm talking about it. I'm telling people without thinking first. That's not what I'm like.' He said to me, 'No, you've become more confident.'

The other change I noticed was that I felt a little bit annoyed. Maybe annoyed is not quite the right word, but I think I felt cheated. It's a little like the anticipation and excitement of going away on a wonderful holiday. When I arrived at this place, I didn't have the anticipation of getting there, because I didn't know I was going, but when I was actually there, there was this excitement of the new world, the excitement that I was breathing, and feeling more alive. It's another world. Everything's kicking on and going on, just like down here. And I was anxious for the next stage; I was very keen to see what was going to happen next. And suddenly it all came to an abrupt end. And then I'm hearing the doctor say that I'm going to hospital. But the wonderful thing about it is, what a great thing I've got to look forward to now! And I can tell you, if anyone told me I was dead I wouldn't have believed it, because I was breathing. I was breathing so well.

I'm also no longer in awe of people. I'm not scared of people anymore. I've become more confident. I see people taking life much too seriously, instead of enjoying the beautiful time that this place is supposed to give them and their family. I honestly believe we're only meant to look after each other and family, and if you don't have family you need to reach out for the ones that need somebody to be there. All the other things in life are incidental. The home's only there to make you comfortable. I almost drink in the beauty of the landscape now. And

I notice every single flower, every tree and I'm very much aware of the weather. I take every single thing in. Car spaces, it's just hilarious. Car spaces are always available to me now! And I talk to the other side now. Any thought that comes into my mind, I don't care whether it's Christian or not now, I don't care less anymore. I like to believe that it's somebody there, and I'm more than happy, if a thought comes into my mind. Not all of them are good, but usually not too bad. It might be somebody getting sick, a sort of warning for me. I've had a few warnings. Hubby's in hospital now, he's alright, but I now have a little bit of preparation. The thought just comes into my mind, and then when it does happen it doesn't seem quite so bad because I've had pre-warning.

And I now often feel that people who have died are with me. They don't appear to me, because I wouldn't be able to cope with that. But I do sometimes feel their presence. I'm aware they are there, but they're quite friendly so I know it's alright.

Jacqueline's story illustrates clearly the changes that often take place in people who have had a near-death experience.

Changes that often take place are:

- Realisation of the need to enjoy every moment of life.
- Becoming less materialistic.
- Being less concerned with the petty things in life.
- Becoming more spiritual. A 'knowing' of what awaits us when we die.
- An understanding of the really important things in life. Like Jacqueline says, 'I honestly believe we're only here to look after each other and family. All the other things in life are incidental.'
- Becoming more confident.
- Loss of fear of death.
- Being aware of the beauty of life.
- Pre-cognitive warnings about events that are about to take place.

- Being more intuitive.
- Awareness that loved ones who have died are still around.

Jacqueline also notes that she wishes she'd had some form of counselling after her near-death experience. This is important as these experiences need to be 'integrated' into our new frame of the world in which we live. For anyone having a near-death experience, their perception of life and death has changed and will never be the same again, so how we make sense of what has happened and how we then conduct our lives as a result of this experience becomes a major factor that needs to be addressed for many people.

One thing is very sure...life is different once you have had a near-death experience, and you cannot help but be touched by the experience.

There is a question that keeps on nagging at me, in the back of my mind. Why is it that of all the people who come close to death, only a small percentage of them will have a near-death experience. Why doesn't everyone who comes close to dying have such encounters?

Well, maybe they do, but just don't remember it. Rick is a friend and fellow hypnotherapist whom I have known for quite some time. His fascinating story raises many questions, highlighting the possibility that we may well all have a near-death experience when close to death, but we simply don't recall the events.

RICK'S STORY

At the end of the year 2000, I underwent urgent surgery that resulted in having five bypasses grafted to my heart. In Intensive Care, soon after the operation, my wife, Margot, stood by my 'lifeless', clammy, and cold form, still unconscious from the anaesthetic. The only way she knew I was still alive, she described later, was from the monitor sounding a steady beep as the green line of its screen bounced with every beat of my heart. She recalls having had a clear impression that this body in front of her was not who I really was. Little did she know how her awareness was about to be tested, for in the next instant my heartbeat ceased and the monitor screamed its alarm into the quiet of the room as I flat-lined.

Margot remembers medicos rushing from all directions as she was hustled out somewhere to a distant waiting room. Over the next hour and a half I was to 'die' twice more before the doctors managed to hold me in my body. Later, as I came out of sedation, there was a great fuss, with people around me asking if I had seen any light or tunnel? I had no idea what they were talking about. I recalled nothing. None of the excitement. No 'near-death experience' we hear so often talked about. Just empty nothingness.

Five years later I was in Santa Fe, New Mexico, participating in some specialised hypnotherapy training with Michael Newton (author of Life Between Lives*) and the Newton Institute, when at dinner one night an instructor, Paul Arnaud, began recounting the story of when both he and his wife were struck by lightning, 'died', and were subsequently revived. She had had a very clear near-death experience, but he, like me, remembered nothing. Six months after Paul's lightning experience, a colleague of Paul's regressed him under hypnosis, where he vividly recollected his own near-death experience! It was recorded in his unconscious mind even though he had not consciously remembered a thing. As you may have guessed, I had a reason for being more than a little interested. I related to him my own earlier close shave with death. I wondered if my non-existent memory of 'dying' could be hiding a near-death experience as well, so he eagerly volunteered to regress me the following day to find out.*

The next morning Paul guided me into a deep trance and, to my amazement, I found myself above my body in the Intensive Care Unit of the hospital, looking down on doctors frantically working to re-enliven my inanimate form. Perhaps I did have a near-death experience after all, I wondered!

In a hypnotic trance one's conscious mind is actually awake and very present, observing the whole experience, something many people do not realise. As I was 'reliving' this experience I was also very aware of my mind protesting, almost screaming in my head, 'What makes you think this is real? You're making this up!' Perhaps it was right.

I was very aware of how these things go, as I regress people every day in my clinic! Yet the instant my conscious mind thought this, I had left the Intensive Care Unit, the medical staff and my body, and found myself deliberately moving through the hospital, directly to a room where Margot was waiting. Not only did I find her sitting on the left hand end of a long, dark sofa, but the fact that I was clearly aware of every thought running through her mind seemed perfectly natural to me.

Then everything started to shift as another awareness arose. A single, highly conscious 'being', I can best describe as light or energy, stood a little behind me, to the side, and slightly raised above me. I became aware of another, and another, until these 'beings' of consciousness and light became quite numerous. While I felt calm and everything appeared totally natural, from here I begin to struggle to explain myself for there are no words that adequately describe what occurred, although I will attempt to.

What I felt can be best described as a welcoming and nurturing, intensely powerful, yet profoundly calm and peaceful presence of absolute acceptance and unconditional love, with a depth that makes everything I have ever experienced before, or since, pale into insignificance.

As I came out of the trance, in that hotel room in Santa Fe, and at the same time the room I visited while also being operated on, I could not help but wonder if any of this was true. It felt so real, but did I make it up? I was keen to find out and there was one person on the planet who could help me.

A few days after the regression, and when the training program in which I was enrolled had been completed, I arrived back at Sydney airport where Margot picked me up. As I closed the car door I could not wait to test my 'recall'. I asked, 'Remember when I flat-lined in hospital and you were bustled out of the Intensive Care Unit and taken somewhere else?' I knew she would. I then confirmed that she had never shared anything of her experience, other than that she was left for an hour and a half to wait to find out whether or not I had survived.

I then relived my experience of a few days earlier, of the twists and turns in the corridors that led to the room she waited in, described what the room looked like, its size, colour, decorations, furniture, that she was sitting on the left hand end of a long, dark couch. I then carefully presented the four significant thoughts running through her mind on that occasion, one at a time. None of this had been discussed before and I was acutely aware that her reply would be like an acid test of the authenticity of existence of life after death. What must have been only a moment felt like eternity suspended in timelessness as I waited for her response.

As we were driving away from the airport she revisited the memory of the day I 'died'. Each and every one of my experiences in trance a few days prior, item by item, corroborated with every one of hers, precisely as I had experienced it in my near-death experience. Then, upon hearing my story a few weeks later, one of our daughters verified the description of the décor and dimensions of the room Margot waited in, including where she had found her sitting on the couch, as she had visited with her there.

I learned at least two invaluable lessons from this experience. One, my tiny sojourn through the veil shed light on the nature of existence beyond death that has left me totally unconcerned about taking my last breath, perhaps even eagerly awaiting it. And two, even more significantly for me, I survived a firsthand experience of the absolute power of moving about as far back from life as possible, and gaining a perspective of the 'big picture', a meaning, a knowing, that how we live counts, that life is about growth. So much of what was once vitally important to me, the drama and issues that plague life, has no real meaning for me now except for how it assists in honing and fine-polishing my ability to raise consciousness, and love absolutely everything about my life.

How many more people who have been close to death actually have had a near-death experience but do not recall the encounter? The use of hypnosis in this area, to my knowledge, has not been explored. I also wonder if this is why some people only experience part of the near-death experience and whether they would recall more details under hypnosis. Interesting isn't it?

MAGIC

One night, quite by magic, whilst I was on holiday with my family, I had the great good fortune to sprain my ankle. Walking from my cousin's place, where we were staying for the night, to her neighbour's where my husband was playing pool, I stepped off her grass on to the neighbouring driveway. I felt a wrenching and tearing feeling as my ankle sickled under me, and down I went. Agony. I waited in the dark whilst my daughter went to get my husband and the much needed ice.

Ice applied, I lay back in the driveway and tried to relax. When the agony that goes along with a sprain finally became a heavy throb I finally opened my eyes. Wow, I was staring at a miracle that we call the Milky Way. My husband and daughter soon followed suit and lay down to keep me, and a few trillion stars, planets and dust, company.

I would have surely missed that precious moment had I not sprained my ankle. And that moment was magic. I will remember it forever. Of course the neighbour whose driveway we were sprawled in thought we were all bonkers. I don't think he had ever seen anything quite like it. I certainly don't think he had ever seen *that* vista from *that* angle of his own driveway.

The Milky Way Galaxy, home to the planet earth, is a mass of stars and planets and gas clouds which span well over a hundred thousand light years of space. It is a massive recycling plant where stars are constantly turning to dust which is re-formed to make new stars. In his wonderful book, *The Universe – A Voyage Through Space And Time*, Nigel Henbest beautifully states, 'Dying stars return gases to the disc (Milky

Way), so topping up the supplies available for making new stars. This has created a cycle of star birth and star death in the disc that could continue for hundreds of billions of years.'

When we look at the stars from our vantage point on earth we are literally looking into the past. We only see the stars how they *were*. The closest star to the earth, the sun, is 92 million miles away. These other little pinpricks we see in the sky at night are much further away. The closest is a cluster of three stars, collectively called Alpha Centauri which is over four light years away. A light-year is the distance light travels in one year, which is about 5.9 trillion miles. Times that by four and that's the closest!

Here's what to do. Arrange to go out somewhere that is away from city lights, a park or clearing where you can lie down and simply look up at the miracle that is the night sky. Pick a clear night. A full moon is spectacular, but a dark moon will ensure a brilliant display of stars.

Star gazing makes for wonderful meditation. It engages our soul and expands our awareness. Spraining your ankle is not mandatory. Take the time to simply *be* with the stars and the planets.

You may know that stars twinkle and planets glow, making it easy to spot the planets. How many planets can you see?

Notice also if you can see any of the constellations.

As you look up at the velvet of night sky just know that it is a mass of birth and death. As above, so below. Stars are constantly in the never ending cycle of being born, living and dying. A staggering 10,000 million years is a mere drop in the ocean.

In your journal, record what you experienced, how you felt, what thoughts went through your mind as you star gazed.

We cannot but be touched by the sheer beauty and magic of a velvet night sky.

Seven

AFTER-DEATH COMMUNICATION

'You expect me to be dead? Come now, Richard.'
'And this is not a dream? I won't forget seeing you now?'
'No. This is a dream. It's a different space-time and any
different space-time is a dream for a good sane earthling, which
you are going to be for a while yet. But you will remember, and
that will change your thinking and your life.'

Illusions - The Adventures of a Reluctant Messiah

Richard Bach

When my dad died I kept wandering around the house not quite knowing where to put myself in order to relieve the pain. The shock, the not believing it could happen, that it is so final, what I should have said, what I shouldn't have said, or done. Feelings of wanting to run away were overwhelming, to somehow get away from the pain and the chaos, but where do you run? There is no getting away from it.

But there was to be a gift, a set of occurrences that would bring about a profound sense of inner peace within me that I could not have imagined possible. There is nothing that helps the healing journey more profoundly and rapidly than the gift of being contacted by a loved one who has died. It is one of the most normal, natural things to happen after the death of someone we love.

With my dad the contact happened fairly rapidly. It was profound and undeniable. It has most definitely changed the way in which I grieve for him. I still miss him terribly, however I know beyond any shadow of doubt that he is just fine.

MY STORY

My dad died peacefully in his sleep, aged 81 years. He had a heart attack, but there was no evidence that he had experienced any pain. I was relieved. I went to collect my mum and my brother and to organise funeral stuff the next day (I only got the call that Dad had died at 11 pm the previous night, and my brother who lives closer went straight around to be with Mum). As soon as I arrived at Mum and Dad's place I knew there was a letter or that there was a 'something' that I had to 'know'. I went through the place like a tornado, looking for that 'something'. After the funeral, when clearing everything out, as Mum was now going to live with us, I again started looking for a letter or 'something'. There was 'something' I had to know. I was completely perplexed as there was no letter. I found nothing.

Over the next few weeks every night as I settled down to sleep I would ask my Dad to visit me in my sleep. Very soon the dreams started. I know that these were more than just dreams as they had a quality about them. I could feel them. In the first dream my dad was in a room without any trappings, just a plain room with a chair, a bed and a window. He was just 'there', he didn't say anything to me, which made me wonder if he had difficulty in communicating. Interestingly, my cousin told me she had been to see a medium who had told her that my dad needed to speak with the person who organises everything in the family (that is most definitely me), but he was having difficulty knowing how to communicate. There was nothing more to this dream, but I was comforted by the fact that it had happened and amazed at how real it felt.

A few weeks later my dad rang me in the middle of the night (I was asleep, but again, it was so real) and said to me very clearly, 'Now, I want you to listen very carefully to me. They won't let me come home.' I immediately thought he thinks he's in hospital, so I said, 'Dad, you're not in hospital, you died.' He replied, 'I know I've died, but they won't let me come home.' Dad used to ring me regularly so it was no surprise and in fact amuses me that he chose this method to get in contact with me. I was delighted that he could now speak to me and that I could hear him.

The next 'contact' came a couple of weeks later, again in my dream. This time I was standing in my parents' bedroom and he came up to me and said, 'I've had difficulty communicating, but it's getting easier. How's this?' and he put his arms around me and gave me a big hug. As he hugged me I had a very strong feeling of what is hard to describe. It felt like pins and needles, but without the numbness. More of a strong, warm tingling feeling. It was so strong and so real. I woke up and could still feel the tingling warmth of the hug. I have to say I was delighted as my dad was a great talker, and I knew it must have frustrated him not being able to communicate. I feel very blessed to have had this experience.

But as it happened there was to be another visit, again only a couple of weeks later. I never knew when it was going to happen, but when it happened it was usually in the early hours of the morning.

This time Dad was standing in a wide corridor. He was holding his hands at right angles to his body, at the base of his neck and at the base of his ribs, saying to me (very animated this time – like he wanted to tell me something very important), 'It's from here (just below his neck) to here (just below his ribs).'

Not understanding, I said, 'Do you think it's indigestion?'

'No, it's not indigestion.'

I said, 'Well could you have pulled a muscle?'

'No, I haven't pulled a muscle! It's like a tight vice around my chest.' And he took hold of my hand, and through his hand I could feel the pulse of his heart beat. I knew in an instant what he wanted to tell me. He was telling me about the heart attack, that he had some chest pain before he died.

I realised at this point that this was one of those 'funny' dreams and that I wasn't dreaming at all. The heart beat I could feel was very, very strong. I was totally aware that I was dreaming and I thought to myself, I'll open an eye and then I'll know I'm not dreaming. And I did, just one eye, and it was bright and sunny. I closed it and drifted for a few minutes more. This was interesting because I sleep with my blinds down. It had been raining for a few days, with no sign of letting up. Consequently when I finally did wake up my room was in darkness, but when I opened my blinds it was bright and sunny – no more rain.

I felt numb and I wondered about this all morning. Didn't speak of it. I couldn't, so profoundly did it affect me. I knew he was telling me about the heart attack, what he had experienced. He always told me things like this, what experiences were like, so it was important to him that I knew exactly what had happened as he had died.

After this, it was to be some time before my dad would contact me again. Finally, once the message was received, there was no need for any further visits. I knew he was okay. I had felt his presence and needed no more. And oddly enough I had a deep inner knowing that it wouldn't happen again for quite some time. It had all brought about an inner peace that I could not have possibly imagined.

This type of experience is what has been called after-death communication. After-death communication was first termed this by Bill and Judy Guggenheim, who conducted research with over 3000 people across America. What they found was that after-death communication was experienced in one form or another by some staggering 20-40% of the population, making it one of the most prevalent of any phenomena surrounding death, including near-death experience. This, however, is probably not a true indication of the prevalence of such experiences as many people never openly admit that they may have been contacted. Fear of ridicule, of such a precious and personal experience being dismissed as trivial, a hallucination due to stress and so forth all go to make disclosure difficult.

The Guggenheims defined after-death communication as a spontaneous event that takes place when a person is contacted directly by a family member or friend who has died.

After-death communication is a most precious gift. It is a gift given to the grieving by the person who has died. The gift's worth is unparalleled, priceless, because it provides comfort to ease the desolate and devastating pain that is felt when someone we love dies. And the effects of this gift can be profound, changing the way in which we grieve, propelling us along the healing journey. It is often reported that, after having such communication, the burden becomes less, we have something to hold on to, something to believe. Not that we miss the person any less, or that we don't feel sad or still grieve. But somehow it is irreversibly changed and is never quite the same again. What a gift!

Anyone can have the experience of an after-death communication. There is no telling when it will happen, sometimes it doesn't happen until years after the death, and often at important times in our lives, when our health is threatened or at some other turning point.

Kathi's father first payed her a visit only two days after his funeral and then again whilst visiting her mother. But it was to be another fourteen years before she was to feel his presence again, at the breakup of her marriage.

KATHI'S STORY

My father and I were very similar in our interests and personalities, and on the weekends during my childhood and teenage years, he would take me to the art galleries and museums, we would sail in his little boat on the harbour, we would surf together and ski together. He was a dare-devil and he taught me to be the same! He would take me down the steepest slopes, onto slippery ice sheets and into white-outs, and we both loved every minute of it!

He developed cancer when he turned sixty, endured shocking pain, and finally, after five years, suffered an agonising death. I was so horrified by the brutality of his death that any faith I had ever had in a loving God was destroyed. Dad had been a good, faithful husband, a wonderful father and the most experienced and respected paediatric endocrinologist in Australia. His patients loved him and he was known as the quiet achiever.

Two days after his funeral, I was making the dinner for my two little boys, and just for a change, I decided to put a small amount of salt on the boys' food before serving it. All of a sudden, out of nowhere, I could feel my father's spirit rush right through me, and a strict message came from him, saying 'Katie, Katie! You'll harden their arteries!' The feeling of his presence only lasted about two seconds, but it was a warm, comforting feeling. I knew he was there and that he hadn't gone forever. Apart from feeling happy, my first thought was, 'How could you be worrying about a small amount of salt on the dinner, after what you've just been through?' But I could also feel the message back that my father's death was over, the pain was irrelevant, as if it had been forgotten completely, that my father was all right, and that I shouldn't worry about him anymore.

About ten days after Dad's death, I was visiting Mum. It was the evening, and as I sat in a chair in the sitting room after dinner, I was aware of Dad's presence, sitting in his usual chair next to mine. He was just sitting there, watching television and being at home, as though he hadn't died and was still there.

I thought a lot after this, and decided that there really was a spirit life after death, that it is not all over when we die, that Dad's spirit had come to comfort me and that maybe even God was there. Since that moment, I have developed a faith and a hope that when we die our spirits are greeted by those of our family and friends who have died before us, and that we join back up with the spirit world.

About fourteen years after Dad died, my husband left me. My three sons were aged nine, fourteen and sixteen. I was going through the traumatic ordeal of dealing with lawyers to sort out a property settlement, and was finding it hard to sleep at night. My blood pressure had gone up and I was feeling very alone and miserable.

In the middle of the night, I was woken from sleep by the sudden presence of my father, with Gran (his mother) standing behind him. I couldn't see this with my eyes. I could just feel it and see it in my mind, as I had with Dad's first visit. I could feel Dad brush my cheek, and I could see the image of me that he had in his own mind. He didn't see me as an adult woman, but as the little four-year-old girl that he remembered. Gran was there to lend support. There was no verbal message, just a quick visit to let me know that they were there and that I wasn't alone. Of course, this experience gave me comfort and helped me to cope a little better.

After-death communications can happen whilst we are awake, sleeping or doing a mundane task such as driving the car or cooking a meal. It seems to be true that if you have had one experience you are quite likely to have several over the course of your life, often, but not exclusively, at significant times. You do not need to be spiritually 'in touch' or have a belief in the afterlife. Often this causes great shock if we do not have a basic belief system in place as we struggle to comprehend what is happening. It simply defies our logical brain because it can't happen, can it?

Children are not exempt from these experiences either, as Chris well knows. Chris was just turning six when his father died from a heart attack during the night.

CHRIS'S STORY

My dad died suddenly at the age of twenty five, in December, 1950, just before my sixth birthday. He had a massive heart attack in bed at 11 pm and was dead before medical help arrived. My memory of this night is of being awakened by the commotion of people crying and running about outside my bedroom door. When the noise subsided, I crept out of my room and into my parents' room, where I discovered two strange men on either side of my dad's bed. One of these men, on seeing me enter the room, started yelling for someone to come and remove me from the bedroom. At this point I saw my father sit up and smile reassuringly at me.

Throughout my life I have been told that this was impossible as he was long dead by this time, but this image is still as clear to me today as it was then, nearly 60 years ago.

Sometimes the visitation can be a shock. Megan had one such fright in the wee small hours.

MEGAN'S STORY

My father and I were very close, but though he had been very unwell for over a year after suffering a series of strokes and was in palliative care, I was not aware that his death was imminent. A couple of days after he died he came to me one night. I know I should say it was in a dream, but it was not a dream. It was the most intense experience. I was asleep in bed when suddenly I sat up as I felt my father's hand on my back. I heard him say, 'I am with you…I will always be with you.' I screamed as it was so intense. I remember my heart was beating very fast. I felt terrified at the time, however I know this was not my father's intention. He just wanted to comfort me.

Very soon after this experience, despite my initial fear, I felt great comfort and I knew my father loved me very much and he just wanted to let me know. It is over twenty years since my father died. I still miss him.

Music is a very powerful and evocative way for contact to be established. A few months after my nephew, Ryan, died, David, Jessica and I were preparing to go to the beach. We were just about ready to leave, when I heard quite a racket going on in our bedroom. I walked down there to discover the TV was turned on, and blaring music was bursting forth. The programme was Rage, a teenage pop music show that none of us watch. Assuming my daughter or husband had turned it on for some reason I said, 'Come on guys, who's turned the TV on? We're about to walk out the door'. They followed me down to the bedroom, shaking their heads. They had most definitely not turned it on. Thinking 'how odd' I turned it off and we went to the beach. Now we rarely go to the beach, perhaps once or twice a year. But when we arrived I commented to David and Jessica that the last time we stood on a beach, on this very beach in fact, we were with Ryan. And then it hit me. Rage was Ryan's favourite programme, he watched it every Saturday morning without fail. This was his way of letting us know he was okay and still around. What are the chances of a TV 'spontaneously' turning itself on to a programme that was so much associated with our deceased nephew at the precise moment we were about to leave for a beach that we had visited with him only a few months prior to his death? I don't think the odds are very good. The TV has never spontaneously turned itself on before or since. I am in awe of this experience.

In this next story, Lyn is awoken by a very special song at the precise moment her father dies.

LYN'S STORY

My dad was on a respirator in Canberra hospital. He had a clot in his lung as well as other lung problems. My mum and family were there every day. After a week or so I had a Christmas party that I wanted to attend and the doctors told me to go, that my dad would still be there when I returned. I felt it was a much needed break from the hospital and stress of it all.

I ride a motorbike, I'm a lady and I live in Sydney. On the Saturday I rode my bike to Swansea for the bike club Christmas party. After the party I made the journey back to my home in order to get a good night's sleep before the journey back to the hospital.

I fell asleep with the radio on. I am unsure how long I was asleep for, but a song eventually woke me. Andre Bocelli, 'Time To Say Goodbye'. It seemed weird. I had never heard that song before until that moment. I immediately picked up the phone and rang the hospital to see how Dad was, and to say I was leaving Sydney shortly. I spoke with the Sister who was crying. She said my dad had just passed away. It was shortly before 5pm. I arrived at my dad's side by 8.30pm that night. I was so very upset under that helmet, and as I rode around Lake George, the sun was setting. There was an incredible feeling of peacefulness. It had been raining, but the sun was shining through the broken clouds with beams of light shining through. I remember feeling that my dad was with me right then.

I had never heard that song before. I feel it was a sign from my dad. I subsequently bought the CD as I wanted this song to be played in the church at his funeral.

The choice of song, the precision with which it was played and the perfect timing of Lyn's awakening is simply astonishing.

Fred seems to have a similar connection through music.

FRED'S STORY

On the 28th of August, 1971, I sold a car to my future wife, Sue, for $370 and she received thirty-six years of after-sales service. Many people knock used car salesmen, but this began a very happy relationship. This date then became our official 'anniversary'.

On August 28th, 1973, I proposed to my wife at the Gap, Watsons Bay. My story is, it was the end of my life as I knew it!

My wife had no real health problems, watched carefully what she ate, and drank very little, the occasional glass of wine.

Carl, my son, and Sue were fascinated with the history of Egypt and watched many documentaries on the subject over quite a few years. They all looked the same to me. But in late 2006, I read about a very attractive tour to Egypt which we eventually booked for the four of us and we planned to leave on 15th March, 2007. Sue went to her doctor for final vaccinations in February, 2007, and she had a cough that wouldn't go away so the doctor gave her an ultrasound which detected a tumour in her liver.

We were told to cancel our holiday and Sue went to hospital on the 15th March 2007, for her first operation to remove this tumour. What appeared to be a small tumour turned out to be fifteen tumours, which then started to spread. At this stage she was in good spirits and you would not have thought she had any problems.

On August 9th, 2007, she went to St Vincents Hospital for a nuclear treatment, exactly thirty years after she went into hospital to have our first child, who was born on the 10th of August, 1977.

Again she was healthy in appearance and attitude but finally accepting the fact that she wasn't getting any better.

A month or so later we were having a drink on the patio and I rather insensitively said that I did not really believe in life after death. Sue started to cry and I said that if she could send me a sign it would be wonderful...

Before her passing, on the 18th of December, 2007, she planned her funeral. It was not religious, but she requested two of her favourite songs to be played at the ceremony – 'The Wonder of You', by Elvis Presley, which she always said was her song, and listening to the words I can understand why.

We regularly drove to the Gold Coast, and sometimes Coffs Harbour, for family holidays and I had recorded quite a few tapes of 'Fred's Favourites' which we played on these occasions. One song, the only song that she would really turn up the volume on, was 'Una Paloma Blanca', a very, very lively song. This song always excited her and she would sing and bounce around in her seat. This was her second choice for her funeral ceremony.

For the last couple of months of my wife's condition I took time off work to look after her as she was deteriorating. I arranged for my head office to purchase a computer for me and set it up to keep me in touch with my business from home whilst I was looking after her.

When Sue passed away my brother came down from Queensland to stay with us for a few days and for the funeral. He taught me how to download music from CDs, iTunes and other sources as I really love music, both modern and ancient. A month or so later I had my sound system updated to play music throughout the house from the computer. As soon as I arrive home from work, and most of my time at hom, I now listen to music from the computer, and radio, neglecting the TV.

These are the signs that I believe Sue has sent to me...

Thursday, 28ᵗʰ of August, our 'anniversary'. Arriving home from work, I turned the computer on and hit the play button, and the first song played was 'The Wonder of You'. This is one chance in the 1643 tunes that I had recorded at this time.

Saturday, 8ᵗʰ November, at 3:15pm. I had been working very hard in the garden and decided to sit down on the patio and have a drink as I was rather exhausted. This is the earliest in the day that I had decided to have a drink since Sue passed away. Again, the first song that played when I hit that button again was 'The Wonder of You', one in 1909 songs at this stage.

Tuesday, 9ᵗʰ December, 2008, as I was getting out of my shower at 9:3 pm 'The Wonder of You' was playing on Radio 2CH. It was then followed by 'Una Paloma Blanca', a hell of a coincidence.

Tuesday, 27ᵗʰ January, 2009. It was my birthday and the music was playing on random. At exactly 7pm, which is normally the time that Sue insisted we have dinner, 'The Wonder of You' again, now one in 2132 songs.

My daughter stayed with me for my birthday weekend and asked me if I ever dreamt of Mum, I replied, 'I know I do, but I don't clearly remember them.' Saturday, 31ˢᵗ January, 2009. I awoke after a dream of my wife that morning and I thought to myself I must tell Kristy, my daughter. At 3pm that day I was about to take my washing to my ironing lady and I remembered the dream I had that morning and thought, I must tell Kristy. As I was leaving the house I turned on my mobile phone and there was a text message from my daughter saying that she had dreamt about Mum the previous night.

Tuesday, 17th February, 2009. 'Una Paloma Blanca', first song to play on the computer after work.

Friday, 20th February, 2009. Coming home late off my train, upon entering my car and turning on the radio, 2CH again, 'The Wonder of You' was being played by Ray Peterson.

Sometimes visits are to deliver a specific message. This is what happened to Chris, whom we met a little earlier in the chapter, when he was visited by his deceased brother.

CHRIS'S STORY

In October, 1997, I lost my brother after a long and stressful battle with cancer. Gary was four years my junior, and although we both had three children, he was blessed with three lovely grandchildren, whilst my kids, even though my youngest daughter was by now married, seemed in no hurry to start a family. Some 15 or 16 months after Gary's death I had a dream one night that Gary had lifted me from my bed and we were flying away together. I suddenly became alarmed and asked was it my time (meaning, to die). *With a big smile Gary said, 'Yes, your turn has come.' Now in a total panic, I started to berate him. It was okay for him as he already had grandchildren, but I was still to see my first. This was unfair. I awoke suddenly and with a jolt, like I had been dropped from a height.*
A couple of days later I received a phone call at work from my daughter informing me she was pregnant. My turn had definitely come!

Sometimes the message is delivered via a third party. In this next story Debbie's deceased uncle needed to communicate with his daughter, using Debbie as the go-between.

DEBBIE'S STORY

In November, 2002, my uncle was diagnosed with an aggressive brain tumour. The doctors removed it to give him two weeks to finalise his affairs and say goodbye to his family and friends. That was all the time he had, and he passed away two weeks later.

His family was left devastated at his sudden death. He was such a healthy, fit man who was only 62 years of age. It didn't seem fair.

In January, 2003, on a warm summer morning, I was dreaming of a party where all the family were present. My uncle was there in the dream — he was wandering around the party feeling concerned. He couldn't speak to me, and the rest of the family couldn't see him.

Knowing how he used to be when he was alive, that he used to always worry about everyone in the family and take it upon himself to look after all of us, I tried to console him by saying, 'It's okay, we're all going to be alright. You can go now and be with my grandmother and grandfather. Don't worry about us anymore.' In the dream I could feel my uncle giving me a big, secure hug. While I was sleeping I could actually feel the weight of his body against mine — that warm secure hug from an uncle.

It was around 5am when I was woken from the dream by the definite weight of a person's body pressing against mine and also the sound of fingers repeatedly strumming on the mattress. The vibration was coming through my pillow. In my groggy state, I reached over to stop my husband's fingers from making the noise. But I found him lying on his stomach, his right hand with the fingers relaxed, facing up into the air and his left hand resting peacefully on his pillow. There was no way he was making the noise!

Suddenly I could feel the presence of someone in the room besides myself and my husband. Gingerly, I opened my eyes to see that there was nothing there and quickly closed them again, as the fear I felt was too much. I didn't want to be afraid as I knew it was my uncle.

So calmly, in my mind, I reassured him that we would all be fine and he needn't worry about us. Only then did the strumming fingers and the vibration stop.

Later that morning, I couldn't get the experience out of my head. I wanted to contact my aunty and tell her, but I was concerned about upsetting her so soon after his death. I just couldn't help myself, I picked up the phone and called her.

I told her of my dream first. I didn't understand the significance of the party...I didn't know what we were celebrating. I told her of the hug he had given me and then I asked her if he ever tapped his fingers in the way I had heard that morning.

Her response blew me away! My uncle had a habit of constantly strumming his fingers over and over. I was unaware of this. He would strum them on the lounge when he was watching TV. He would strum them over the keys in his pocket. He would strum them on the steering wheel in the car. I knew then that he was letting me know it was him in the room by showing me his sign.

I continued to chat to my aunty and asked her if she was doing anything special that day. She told me that it was her daughter's 30th birthday. My cousin was very close to her dad. They were having to celebrate her birthday without him, so it was going to be a difficult day for all of them.

Now I knew why I dreamt of the party! It was for my cousin! And since I am not particularly close to her, I didn't know it was her birthday or that it was a special age birthday. My uncle had come to me to let them know that he was concerned that they thought he wasn't going to be there for his daughter's birthday. It all made sense!

Then I questioned why he picked me out of all the family to communicate with. As it turned out my uncle had been trying to make contact with my aunty but she was taking heavy doses of sleeping tablets to help her sleep at night. A psychic had told my aunty to stop taking sleeping tablets as my uncle often sat on the end of her bed at night, trying to reach her, but she wasn't able to feel his presence due to her deep state of sleep.

The dream message all made sense now. I had done what I was supposed to do. I'd made contact with my aunty and let her know that my uncle was going to be there with them on that special day.

And sometimes, there is no message at all. It is as though the visit is simply to bring comfort. Here is one such beautiful story.

JENNY'S STORY

I had a strange dream about a month after my mother died. It was definitely more than just a dream. In this dream she owned a small antique shop (antiques were her favourite things). We were having a cup of tea together in her shop and were deep in conversation about how best to look after my father now that she had gone. Then I asked her how she was, and she got upset and suddenly disappeared. The dream was over. It was like a snippet of a conversation we'd been having and, although we were deep in conversation about my dad, I cannot remember the contents of the conversation. Very strange. I thought it was so sweet about the antique shop, she just loved them and her hobby was buying and selling them. I find it interesting that she left when I asked how she was. There are some things we just don't understand. But it was very comforting.

Visitations are not exclusive to humans either. Our furry friends are just as likely to pay us a visit. I have had dogs for most of my life, but only one has ever visited. It was to become a frequent occurrence.

MY STORY

I work from home, and see clients in a home office. When Rosie was alive, if I had spent a particularly long time with any one client, she would put her nose to the bottom of the outside of the door and sniff. I often used to hear her and sometimes I'd let her in, much to the delight of my clients — she was very cheeky and cute. After she died it was quite a common occurrence for this to still happen. I would be working with a client and I would hear a sniff under the door. The first time it happened I thought my husband must have come home and let our other dogs in, which we kept in a separate part of the house, then I started to panic, because I knew my husband hadn't let them in because he wasn't home, and thought a burglar must have let them in. But none of this had happened. The sniffing under the door when I had spent a long time with a client continued for about a year and I just had to get used to it.

Often our loved ones just want to say their final farewells as they depart.

KYLIE'S STORY

I was very close to my 88-year-old grandmother. I spent a lot of time with her as I was growing up, and have also inherited many of her strong traits! 'Old Nanny', as my kids referred to her, was a very determined and independent woman. She still lived on her own, ran her house and went about her daily routine as if she was 20 years younger. It was only within the last 18 months of her life that she had stopped mowing her lawn twice a week, finally accepting help. She still tended to her garden daily. As she was an early riser, she would often begin in the cool hours of the morning before the sun was too hot.

Early one morning, a neighbour saw her kneeling and pulling weeds at 6.30am. Another neighbour passed by some three hours later and, when she did not respond to his greeting, came closer to see how she was. Old Nanny was found to have suffered a severe stroke. She was hospitalised where she suffered a series of small heart attacks.

To see such an independent strong-willed woman suddenly incapacitated was extremely hard for all of our family. She would communicate with her eyes and we knew how very hard, in fact torturous, it was for her to not be able to talk or move.

Early one morning I had a very vivid dream of Old Nanny. I had not previously dreamt of her throughout her illness, or even before that. In this dream she came to me clearly saying goodbye. She left saying she loved me. I was then woken by the phone ringing. It was my mother saying Old Nanny had died.

I knew my grandmother had visited me as she left. I was open to this and was not surprised to have been contacted by her. What really surprised me was that, later in the morning, my mother received a call from one of my grandmother's closest friends, saying she had had a vivid dream at around 5am that morning. In the dream Nan had come to say goodbye. It was only then that my mother told her that she had passed away. Nan had also visited her friend on her final journey home.

Unless you have experienced the death of a loved one by suicide you cannot even begin to understand the full range of anguish that family members may experience. Doug shares his very beautiful and moving story about his son's tragic death by suicide.

DOUG'S STORY

I would like to share a personal experience regarding my son, Andrew, which has had a profound effect on my life. Andrew was attending a secondary college in Moree NSW and was in Year 12. He was quite popular, happy-go-lucky and envied by many for his popularity.

At this time in my life I owned and operated a bus company with Ministry of Transport contracts.

One week prior to my son's death I heard a voice speaking to me, telling me that there was going to be a death in the Shepherd family, a large funeral or maybe even the biggest funeral this community had ever seen. After being told this I assumed it was going to be me, because I was driving on the roads all the time.

Tuesday, 20ᵗʰ July, 1999. Work with the buses always started at approximately 5.45am, which was the case this particular morning. Returning to the depot at about 9.10am, I was surprised to find my son's car still parked at the front of the premises as he should have been at school. As I approached the vehicle I heard the radio playing, and as I bent in through the window to switch it off, I noticed a knife on the seat and a letter beside it. This being out of character, I looked around and, to my alarm, I was confronted with my son's body hanging from a rope in front of me. Many things cross your mind at a time such as this, but my immediate reaction was to grab a ladder and quickly check to see if there was anything I could do. But of course it was too late.

I looked into his eyes and asked God to bless him and take care of him, not blame him or anyone else for my loss.

Wednesday, 21st July, 1999. Approaching the bus shed at about 5.45am, I saw a misty form floating around in the shed where Andrew's body had been found. To me this was Andrew, in spirit form, giving me comfort.

Thursday, 22nd July, 1999. Andrew's sisters arrived home from the Gold Coast and were taken by police, and the doctor, to the mortuary to see his body with the rest of the family, excluding me as I didn't want to see him in his present state.

Friday, 23rd July, 1999. Funeral day. I asked God to give me strength and courage. Whilst three of Andrew's teachers were reading his eulogy, one of my daughters and myself saw two big angels, with wings, at least six or seven foot high, come down from the top of the church and stand beside them (the teachers). I then noticed a misty form appear, like the one I had seen previously in my shed.

Friday evening 8.35pm. My daughters were sitting in the lounge room beside an open fire. I was fairly tired so I decided to retire to the bedroom for a while. After laying there for 10 minutes I placed my hands under my head, lying on my back and said, 'Lord I know my son is in heaven. Can I see him?' A second or two later, with my eyes shut, I entered into a black tunnel. Upon entering I could see this small white light in the centre. As I travelled towards it I could see some high yellow lights on the edges of the tunnel. As I arrived at this light, which only took a matter of seconds, it seemed so high and bright that I couldn't look directly at it, but at a 45 degree angle. I *thought this must be God or heaven or whatever, so I thanked God for showing me where my son was. Then to the right of this light I could see my son from the waist up, dressed in a robe with a big smile on his face. The only thing about him that appeared different was the amount of hair on one side of his head, there seemed to be not much of it. I immediately thanked God for my vision and went to tell my daughters about what had just happened. I commented about Andrew's hair, and they then told me that when they had visited the mortuary they were informed by the funeral director that he had cut some of Andrew's hair off for my wife and myself. As I mentioned earlier, I had not been to the mortuary and I did not know that any hair had been cut off. I had no idea.*

Monday morning, 26th July, 1999. I arrive home to find visitors wanting to chat. After having a quick coffee, I mentioned to them that I needed a rest because at 10.30am I needed to go and pay the funeral director. I went for a rest and lay down. I asked God to give me the strength to get through the day. Immediately, I felt something like a stick or spear go into my ribs on the right side of my body. Then pins and needles in my right hand, followed by a huge amount of heat rising up my right arm and into the rest of my body.

I jumped up off the seat and went to tell my friends what had happened. I just had so much energy, I was then able to go off and pay the funeral director and carry on with the rest of the day.

Whatever the reason for the visitation, whether it is to bring comfort, to give a message or to simply say one final goodbye, once you have experienced such a contact it stays forever in your memory and you never forget it. It is indelibly woven into the fabric of your being. It stays with you for the rest of your life. And you *know* it's real.

People who are bereaved often have a great need to share the wonderment of their experience with others, needing some validation for what has happened, but many do not for fear of ridicule or of their precious, priceless experience being dismissed or discounted. It is important that if you are a family member supporting someone who is experiencing grief that you understand that these experiences are so very real. Be supportive even if you don't believe it yourself. Until you have had such an experience yourself it can be a difficult concept to grasp. After-death communications hold tremendous power to bring about positive changes for the bereaved, reducing fear and anxiety and promoting a sense of peace at the time of utter chaos that is grief.

Stories such as these touch us at the very core of our being. They give us hope, and change the way in which we grieve. They tell us something about the mysterious journey into death which we must all undertake and give clues about what may lie beyond. They also resonate deep inside each and every one of us, and touch our soul in a very special way.

I will conclude this chapter now with a beautiful story from Julia that highlights the incredible synchronicity that often surrounds dying.

JULIA'S STORY

My aunt suffered a stroke nearly 10 years ago. I received a phone call from her neighbour telling me that she was very unwell, so I went to her unit. I met the doctor there and then waited with her until the ambulance arrived to take her to hospital. It was suggested, by the ambos, that I did not accompany her. So the next day, Saturday, I visited her in hospital. She looked so much better than she had the night before and, apart from having difficulty swallowing, she was sitting up in bed and looking her usual, gorgeous self. I visited her again on Sunday and she seemed even stronger, so I assumed that it would be a repeat of her previous stroke procedure. Thinking that she would have a week in hospital, a week or two in a convalescent home then go back to her unit, I told my aunt that I had a particularly busy few days and asked if it would be okay if I visited her on Wednesday. She said that was fine and that she would look forward it.

Mum visited her on Monday and rang to say she was doing well. She visited her again on Tuesday but my aunt's condition had deteriorated. Mum had decided to wait until my aunt's condition improved, before telling me. When I rang Mum on Wednesday morning, she told me that her condition had worsened and the hospital had rung and said that her night had not been a good one. I was cross that she had not rung and told me the day before, as I would have found time to visit after work. I was a preschool teaching director and I worked from 8.30- 4.00 every day.

As soon as I got off the phone, a voice in my head said, 'If you leave work at 4.00 today and then visit the hospital it will be too late!' I immediately rang one of my teaching assistants and asked her if she could change her shift from 10.00-2.00 to 12.00 till 4.00, as I was leaving early. She said she could.

I left Kindergarten at 3.15 and got to the hospital at 3.45. I drove up and the parking attendant was in the booth. I panicked and stammered, 'I am so sorry, I have absolutely no money with me.' He smiled and told me not to worry but to go through to the parking area anyway! I was very appreciative but amazed. I found a perfect parking spot, about the only one in the whole car park.

I went up to my aunt's room and found she was unconscious, with an oxygen mask on and a feeding tube in her nose. I was obviously upset and the nurses were wonderful, kind, supportive and thoughtful. After a few minutes, I bent over her and gave her kisses and cuddles and then whispered, ' This is not fair, after all you have done for me and the family, you don't deserve this. If you are ready to let go, it's okay. We love you, I love you. Thank you for all you have done for me. I love you very much.' I then went out to the nurses' station and asked if there was a priest in the hospital. They assured me that they could find one, which religion did I want? I said I was Catholic but my aunt was Church of England, but I was sure that she would not mind. A few minutes later the priest arrived. He was my aunt's priest from the church she had attended for over 30 years. He just happened to be visiting and was on that floor! I had heard so many wonderful things about him, and my aunt had talked to him about me but we had never met. We were both surprised, and chatted about my aunt enthusiastically.

I asked if he could say a prayer. He held her hand, and I stroked her forehead and I watched the pulse in her throat. During the prayer she died. When the prayer finished I said, ' She's gone, she died during the prayer,' It was 4.15.

I rang the buzzer and the nurses came straight in. I told them what had happened and they were amazed and said it could not have been more perfect had we planned it. As my husband says, 'Sometimes all the holes in the Swiss cheese line up!' It had been one of those occasions.

I was obviously very sad, not scared, not spooked or frightened, just so sad that she was gone, but so very grateful that I had been there. I was also very relieved that I had listened to that 'voice'. My husband thinks she had willed me to be there. Someone or something certainly had.

On the Saturday which followed, we were at a school rowing regatta, a group of six rowers, who were also in the pipes and drums band, including our son, who played the bagpipes. It was lovely and as I looked up I saw my aunt, smiling at us. She was only there for a short time but looked so relaxed and happy. Then she was gone. I could not stop smiling as I told my husband what I had just seen. The experience filled me with such love and happiness.

The funeral was the following week and our son played the Cradle Song for her. It was a very moving tribute to our wonderful and loving aunt.

Eight

HOW TO RESPOND

God answers sharp and sudden on some prayers,
And thrusts the thing we have prayed for in our face,
A gauntlet with a gift in it...

Elizabeth Barrett Browning

S o just how should we respond when a family member shows signs
of nearing-death awareness, or suddenly begins to communicate
with someone who has been dead for some time? What about after-
death communication: how do you react when your friend tells you
they have been visited by, or seen and spoken to, their deceased
mother during the early hours of the morning? What do you say to
Uncle Harry when he tells you he's seen the light at the end of the
tunnel during his operation?

I know I was in shock when my dad first told me that his brothers
had visited. And a part of me thought perhaps it was his medications
that had caused this, as I tried to rationalise what had happened.

But there are in fact many documented cases all with a similar flavour, and in hindsight the symbolism of what took place was just too strange, too close to the knuckle. I know also that I was alarmed, as I thought that he was probably going to die very soon, although he was still coping quite well with day-to-day stuff. It is often one of those moments when you want to jump in and tell them, 'Oh, it's your medication, it's stress, it's...'

Here are some basic guidelines to assist you if you have been fortunate enough and trusted enough for a friend to share their experience with you.

LISTEN

Listen carefully to what they are telling you. Be present. Stop what you are doing and listen. Remember they are sharing something with you that is very real to them. These experiences are fascinating and very special. They deserve your attention.

REFLECT BACK

Reflect back to them what you have heard. This allows them to feel that you understand.

DON'T JUDGE

Move your own stuff out of the way. Don't judge, try to rationalise, or fit it into any model of religion.

DISCOVER MEANING

Allow them to tell you what they think it means, but give help if you see a clear symbolic message. They may not be able to see the symbolism, as in the case with my dad. Help them to find meaning in their experience.

BE ACCEPTING

Don't preach, sweep it under the carpet or be dismissive. If you do, they won't tell you the next time it happens. Be accepting of what they are sharing with you. It is very special. There is so much that we just don't understand. Let them know that you believe them.

DON'T OFFER LOGICAL EXPLANATIONS

These experiences are spiritual in nature and are beyond logic.

DON'T PREDICT OUTCOMES

In the case of nearing-death awareness, don't tell them it means they are going to die. It may not be the case. There are many documented cases where the person has been near to death at the time of the nearing-death awareness and then recovered.

ACKNOWLEDGE THE TRUST

Let them know how important it is to you that they have chosen to share this experience with you. It means that they trust you.

The plethora of stories presented here in Part 2, are *The Reality*. These are *normal* people having *normal* experiences. And the truth is we can all draw back the thin, gossamer veil that separates the living from the dead. The slightest breeze and it lifts, just enough for us to know and understand. We can no longer hide from what *is*.

Because nearing-death awareness, near-death experiences and after-death communications are a subjective experience, they cannot be scientifically tested, cannot be reproduced in any way in a laboratory. This is problematic to science because science is blinkered when it comes to any subjective experience. It has, to date, no way of measuring or quantifying anything that cannot be objectively measured or tested. And sadly, what doesn't fit into this limited view is simply dismissed.

Our society is also geared up for physical reality. We tend to operate and orient to materialism. We drive a car, go to work, make money and pay the mortgage. We fight with the wife, the husband, the boss. We wear watches so we can keep to time, which may or may not exist, according to some scientists. We are literally bogged down in advertising, bombarded with news, bombs going off, shootings, and on and on it goes. Science determines what is real and what is not. In order to exist it must be measured, calculated, test-tubed or cultured. So when a non-physical experience comes along, many shake their heads and tut-tut, because it quite simply doesn't fit into anything else we relate to on a daily basis.

But in order for us, and science, to move forward from this limited way of viewing the world we need to let go of our need to dismiss subjective experiences and accept that there does indeed seem to be something else going on, some other reality that appears non-physical in nature. Ask anyone who has been bestowed with a nearing-death awareness or after-death communication, or a near-death experience for that matter, and they will tell you quite categorically that it is absolutely real. No doubt whatsoever.

But science, whilst mostly unprepared to comment on the phenomena of death, does offer up some very interesting insights. Before we move into the cerebral realms of the next destination on our journey, The Science, take a few moments to visit the Temple of Solitude.

THE TEMPLE OF SOLITUDE

You might like to ask a trusted friend to read The Temple of Solitude aloud to you, or alternatively record your own voice. Ensure that there is a long pause between each passage to allow you the time to follow each instruction.

We all have a wise part of ourselves, an inner part that is intuitive. Some people call it our inner wisdom or higher self. Some call it an angel or higher being. It's time to meet with this wise being.

Find a comfortable place to sit or lie. Take the phone off the hook or whatever you have to do to ensure you are not disturbed.

Take a few moments to just let go with all of your body. If you have any thoughts that are distracting also simply observe them and let them go too. If you are feeling uptight or anxious in any particular place in your body then just allow your awareness to move there and breathe peace into this place.

And when you are ready just imagine or pretend for a moment that you are at the side of a large body of water, a lake. And the surface of the lake is smooth. It's almost like glass. The moonlight reflected off the lake is almost dazzling, a ribbon of light shimmering, connecting one side of the lake to the other.

And gliding towards you is a small boat. You step inside, quite safe, and the ferryman rows you across to the other side. He knows exactly why you are here and where you are going. The water laps around the little boat as it moves gently towards the island on the opposite shore. Notice the gentle rocking motion as you take a moment to allow yourself to relax even further.

You step ashore, knowing that the ferryman will wait for you. You climb the marble steps to the temple, moonlight acting as a lantern, showing you the way.

This is the Temple of Solitude.

As you enter you notice that it has no roof, but is perfectly canopied by a few million stars and a bright silvery moon. Instinctively you know where you need to go. Walk along the labyrinth of corridors until you find exactly the right chamber. Inside you notice that there is a figure standing in the centre of the room; this could be a higher part of yourself, or some other being that is infinitely wise. As you enter into this part of the temple notice the love and peace and understanding and healing that is emanating from this wise one. Just take a moment to really feel this as it enters into your body, into your mind.

You find a place to sit, a place to simply be with the wise one, a place where you can just rest for a while and enjoy the peace, the love, the understanding and the healing that is being offered to you. Notice as these beautiful feelings enter into your body filling it with as much love, as much peace, as much understanding and healing as you need at this moment. This is the gift your wise one offers and it is limitless, eternal, infinite.

You can take this opportunity to ask your wise one any question you want. Think for a moment what it is you would like to ask. Know that the answer may be given in the form of a word, or a picture, or a memory or indeed a symbol. The answer may come much later, in a dream or maybe in a feeling of peace as you go about your business later in the day. Whether you receive the answer now or later is irrelevant; just ensure you listen carefully for your answer. It will come. Pay attention.

You can stay in the temple of solitude for as long as you need and just know that you may also return here as often as you wish. The healing gifts your wise one holds are infinite and are yours to receive at any time.

When it is time for you to leave, embrace this wise soul and thank them for the gifts of love and peace and understanding and healing. These are priceless jewels beyond measure.

Make your way back down the path, leaving behind you the temple of solitude still basking in the moonlight. The ferryman is waiting, just as you knew he would be. You board the small boat and again notice the gentle rocking motion of the boat and the lapping of the water.

Smoothly you leave the boat and the ferryman returns once more from whence he came.

When you are ready take a nice deep breath and bring your awareness back into the room.

Take a few moments to reflect on what has taken place and, when you are ready, record this in your journal. Be aware that the answer to your question may not happen immediately, it may unfold with your day. It may come as a sudden flash of insight, or the answer may come from a friend or through a dream or even perhaps in a book you are reading. It may be that an issue just suddenly resolves itself or that the pieces of a puzzle just fit into place. Record anything you feel is appropriate or associated with this experience.

Part 3

THE SCIENCE

If an elderly but distinguished scientist says that something is possible he is almost certainly right, but if he says that it is impossible he is very probably wrong...

Arthur C Clarke

BLIND

The bright light of the rising sun woke the boy up. He stirred, tentatively opened his eyes and looked around. Only ash was left from the fire that had burned so intensely the night before. Sitting up he turned his head in every direction. He was alone. Everybody was gone. His memories were confused. *The old lady was there, people telling of their stories,* he mused. *I do not remember all the details but I know that their stories will be with me forever.* Rubbing his eyes, his thoughts went back to the black powder. *I thought I would remain blind forever. It is true that when you are blind to the outside, you can listen with your heart. I should remember that.* His thoughts continued.

The boy got up, picked up his bowl and his wolf skin and wondered what to do next. He noticed that at the opposite end from where he came in there was another opening in the wall. With his head still full of the voices he had heard during the night, the boy started walking, alone once again. Only this time he felt better, lighter than before.

There is a difference between being alone and feeling lonely, the boy thought. He had left his hut only a few days ago, and he had learned so much already. *Today I am alone, but after last night I know that I will never be lonely again,* he told himself. That thought made him feel even better, and he started the rest of his journey with a light heart.

As the boy's mind was still busy reliving the beautiful stories of last night, he noticed a man walking with a long piece of wood in his hand. While his head was lowered towards the ground, he swiped the stick from right to left in front of him. The boy was transfixed; he had never seen anybody do that before. He stood there and waited as the man approached.

As the man drew closer to him, he stopped and for the first time he lifted his head and nodded in the general direction of the boy saying, 'Who is there? Who are you?'

The boy gasped and could not reply. Looking in the old man's face he saw that where the eyes should have been was empty. Two empty sockets covered by a thin membrane. The boy instinctively took a step back and almost fell.

'Who's there? Why don't you speak? What do you want?' the man repeated.

The boy took a deep breath and found the words to reply, still fixated on the man's eyes. 'I am a boy wandering alone. I do not seek anything from you.'

But the man did not believe him. 'Everybody wants something. And usually something that belongs to someone else!'

The boy was confused. *Yesterday was the old woman, and today the old man. It's like everybody speaks in riddles,* he thought. But aloud he said, 'I do not want anything from you. Who are you? What happened to your eyes?'

The man leaned on the stick he was carrying and said, 'My eyes were lost when I was young. Where do you come from?'

The boy replied, 'From the forest just behind the hills. I lived by myself and I decided to go on a journey.' After a small pause he added, 'Where do you come from?'

The man ignored the boy's question and went on, 'Nobody lives alone in a forest. I don't believe you! Where are you going?'

The boy was puzzled; he had never met anyone like this man before. 'I do not know where I am going. I am searching for something that was lost to me and will go wherever my journey takes me in order to find it. But last night I did meet some interesting people. And an old lady,' he added. He so wanted to share with someone what had happened to him last night.

'Liar! Nobody lives in this part of the world. I have been here all my life and I have never met an old lady, nor any group of people hereabouts.' The man went on, 'You are trying to make a fool of me.'

The boy did not know what to say next. He did not understand the man's behaviour. 'What reason would I have to lie to you? I have nothing to gain.' The boy was getting tired of this conversation, and for the first time in his life he actually wished he was alone.

Weighing the boy's words, the old man said, 'Tell me about these people that you speak of.'

The boy took a deep breath, and with a river of words he did not know he possessed, he told of what he remembered of the stories. It felt so good to be able to share them with someone. *After all*, the boy thought, *this man cannot see, so he should be able to listen with his heart*.

When the boy had finished the telling of his stories the man shuffled on his feet, shifting his weight a little. Intimidatingly, he said, 'Liar, what proof do you have of any of it?'

Looking at the blind man the boy felt sadness inside. He was not sure where the words came from, but he did not hesitate in saying them. 'When I first met you a moment ago I was sad for your blindness. Now I am only saddened for your deafness. You ask for proof, but your mind is already busily creating reasons to reject it. It does not matter what I tell you as proof, you would not accept it.' What had the old lady said the night before? 'Listen with your heart and you will hear.' This man was not listening with his heart.

'What happened to your eyes?' the boy insisted.

'Nothing that would be of interest to you, boy,' replied the man.

'What happened to your eyes?' the boy would not let go, 'because what made you blind also made you deaf. What happened to your eyes?'

'When I was young my father brought home a wild eagle. He said that it was safe for us to come near it. But, as you can see for yourself, it was not.' The man's voice was almost a whisper, sadness softly sprinkling his words like raindrops.

The boy understood the man. He could not trust. It made sense, even to a young inexperienced boy like himself. He could feel the sadness in the man like it was his own. He also knew, instinctively, that there was nothing he could do for him. This man was on his own journey, for his own purpose, seeking out proof in order to reject it. In his own way, he was also looking for his own shadow.

The boy stood in front of the man, touched his hand with his own, and said, 'I hope that one day you will find your shadow, because when you find your darkness you will also find your light. When you start listening with your heart you will hear.' And without saying another word the boy left the man standing there. There was nothing else he could say.

The boy did not know where he was going, but he was on a journey nevertheless. Today he had learned a new lesson, probably the most important so far. Just because something cannot be proved does not mean that it did not happen.

While his mind was busy thinking, his heart was listening. As the boy kept walking away a new thought came into his mind that almost made him stop. *I am free now. When you no longer care if you are believed or not then you are free.* And he continued his journey feeling good, and free.

Nine

FRINGE-DWELLERS

Every truth passes through three stages before it is recognised.
In the first, it is ridiculed.
In the second, it is opposed.
In the third, it is regarded as self-evident.

The Ignorance of Science

Arthur Schopenhauer

W hen it comes to the phenomena of nearing-death awareness, near-death experiences and after-death communications, there are many different brain based and psychological theories, most dismissing the idea that the soul or spirit survives after death, instead claiming that these experiences are the hallucinations of a dying or traumatised brain. Most physicians, psychologists and scientists are still in the first stage of the 'ignorance of science' - ridicule. Like the old man in the story, they blindly dismiss what they cannot prove.

Because these experiences do not fit into the current paradigm, do not fit into what is accepted about the physiological and psychological brain as we know it, it is an area that is largely ignored by mainstream science. It will probably remain so for some time, as the paradigm shift required to entertain a notion of the possibility of consciousness or spirit surviving death would turn the scientific world on its head.

There are, however, some very courageous doctors and scientists, fringe dwellers though they may be, with curious and enquiring minds, who are sitting up and taking note of these experiences. Dr Sam Parnia is one of these.

Dr Parnia is Fellow in pulmonary and critical care medicine, founder of the Consciousness Research Group and chairman of the Horizon Research Foundation, established to raise funding for large scale research into the near-death experience in cardiac patients: in particular, cardiac patients who flatline during cardiac arrest and report they have had a near-death experience at a time when there is no electrical signal in the brain. That is, they are brain dead at the time of the near-death experience. Within the current paradigms of science this is technically impossible. If there is no electrical signal in the brain then it is not possible for there to be any coherent thoughts or laying down of memories. Dr Parnia is indeed a most courageous man and I look forward to monitoring his work in this area.

A wonderful book springs to mind called *Recovering The Soul – A Scientific and Spiritual Search* by Larry Dossey M.D. One theory proposed by Larry Dossey is that mind is 'nonlocal' to body, a theory first put forward by Rupert Sheldrake, another such fringe dweller in the scientific world. Dr Dossey states 'Sheldrake's hypothesis is relevant to our idea of nonlocal mind, with which it is most compatible. His (Rupert Sheldrake) idea of formative causation suggests that the human mind is nonlocal in both space and time; that it is not confined to the here-and-now; that it is nonmaterial and nonenergetic, implying that its effect is not diminished by spatial separation.' He goes on to say, 'It is neither confined to the brain nor produced by it, although it may act *through* the brain, much as electricity acts through a wire without being generated by the wire itself.'

There are many wonderful books about the theories behind these phenomena, many of which I will list at the end of this book. They are worth exploring and make for very interesting reading. It is not my endeavour here to bring you other people's theories in any great depth, so I will leave you to explore them when you are ready to do so.

But let's have a quick look at what is known about the brain.

REFLECTION

Just take a moment to reflect on what you have read so far. We have indeed come a long way on the journey. I know that I am overwhelmed by the stories that people have submitted along the way. These are stories of love, of connection, of a reality where death does not mean the end of relationship.

In her wonderful book, *The Infinite Thread*, US psychotherapist Alexandra Kennedy tells us, 'Death need not cut us off from those we love. Through dreams and techniques using the imagination, we can access an inner relationship with a deceased loved one, a relationship that offers powerful and mostly untapped opportunities for healing, resolution and even guidance.'

Consider the magnitude of this. Think for a moment what this might be like, you and your loved one, souls that are not 'cut off' but always connected. Turn this over in your mind so that you too may be able to do this.

In your journal make a list of all the benefits of actively engaging in this relationship.

Ten

BRAINWAVES

Let the mind be enlarged, according to its capacity, to the grandeur of the mysteries, and not the mysteries contracted to the narrowness of the mind...

Sir Francis Bacon

Okay, let's keep this nice and simple. If we just imagine for a moment that the mind is a computer. The conscious mind, the convoluted cortical regions of your brain, is the part that you do your thinking with. Using the computer analogy, it's the software. It's the part of your brain that is actively involved in thinking about, interpreting and making sense of the words you are reading right now. It allows you to analyse incoming data from your senses and make deductions in order to work things out. Your conscious mind can only hold about six or seven bits of information at any one time, which is why as you read this you are probably not aware of, say, the birds twittering outside your window. You might be aware of some peripheral visual stimulation and perhaps some sounds around you, but mostly it will go unnoticed.

The internal hard drive of our computer is what is called the *sub*conscious mind, which is located deep in the limbic system of the brain. The subconscious, unlike the conscious mind, can do any infinite number of tasks without you even being aware that it is doing so. And it is because it is below your level of awareness that it is called *sub*conscious. It controls body functions such as breathing, heartbeat, body temperature, thirst, sex drive, the flight or fight response and so forth. The limbic system is also where all our emotions are generated from and where all long-term memories are stored.

There are many misconceptions regarding brain function. It has been said that we only use 10% of our brain's full capacity, but in nature if you don't use a particular part of the body it atrophies and eventually over time becomes redundant. This would cause our brain to shrink. In actual fact, this is not the case. The human brain has continued to get bigger over thousands of years. This indicates that we are actually using the full capacity of our brain; otherwise we would simply lose it. I liken it here to a radio. When you turn on your radio you are using 100% capacity of the unit. You can turn the radio down low, but you are still using 100% of the function of the radio unit. Positron emission tomography (PET) brain imaging scans show that we actually do use all areas of our brain. We may only use certain parts for certain activities and processing. Just like when you use your muscles, you don't necessarily use all muscle groups in every activity, but during the course of the day all muscles do get used.

The brain constantly produces electrical signals, called brain waves or frequencies. Brain waves radiate through the skull and can be detected by what is called an electroencephalogram or EEG. Our brain waves affect the level of consciousness we experience, are constantly fluctuating and can be measured in frequencies or cycles per second, also called hertz.

Brain monitoring shows us that during normal waking state our brain waves oscillate somewhere in the region of 14 to 40 cycles per second. The more anxious we become the higher the frequency. This is what scientists call Beta consciousness.

But during relaxation, meditation, daydreaming and hypnosis these frequencies slow down to around 7 to 14 cycles per second. A reasonable level of trance or depth of meditation is reached at around 7 cycles per second. This level of consciousness is called Alpha. It is Alpha state that we pass through every night when we go to sleep and also briefly whilst waking up in the early hours of the morning. When we are tending to a mundane task, such as watching television, reading a book, washing the dishes and so forth, this also, because of the 'mundane-ness' of the task, is slightly trance inducing. In other words the brain waves slow during these times. This is why some communications happen during these times. Alpha state is very conducive to after-death communication experiences, when we are relaxed, not quite awake, but not quite asleep, in that in-between phase or tending to some mundane task.

The next level of brain frequencies is called Theta. In Theta oscillations of the brain occur at about 3.5 to 7 cycles per second. Deep relaxation, deep hypnosis, sleep and dreams all happen here. It is here also that some after death-communications may occur. And whilst we may well be asleep, people often report that their visitations were not just a dream but had a very real quality to them.

Delta frequency happens between 0.25 and 3.5 cycles per second. Deep slow-wave sleep happens here. Heart rate and breathing are slow and regular. Someone who is in the delta phase of sleep is hard to awaken. Coma also happens here. Not a great deal is known about coma, it is not fully understood, but it appears that the body shuts down much of its functioning, often in order to heal itself. Although we tend to lose awareness at these deep levels it has been shown that some people in coma can actually still hear what is being said to them. This is where many near-death and out-of-body experiences may occur.

After-death communications often occur during sleep, or whilst doing a mundane task. As we have seen, brain wave patterns change during these times, and it is this very change in brain patterns that creates the perfect environment for an after-death communication to occur. Most after-death communications, if not all, occur during this 'altered' state.

So, the important thing to remember here is that the brainwaves we may experience at any one given moment fluctuate constantly. It is when we enter the Alpha or Theta states that nearing-death awareness and after-death communication occurs. The Delta (unconscious) state is where most, if not all, near-death experiences occur.

Enough said about the brain, let's have a look at what quantum physics has to say...

Eleven

QUANTUM PHYSICS

Energy cannot be created or destroyed,
it can only be changed from one form to another...

Albert Einstein

Quantum physics offers us some interesting theories that seem to lend more understanding and flexibility in terms of our comprehension of consciousness and what happens when we die.

I am no physicist and I do not pretend to understand quantum physics. But it has been said that no one understands quantum physics. So with this in mind, I'll attempt to explain in simple, no jargon, terms. A thousand pardons in advance for any errors in interpretation. I attempt here to stick to the basics and give an overview. I would recommend that you research further if you are interested in this fascinating area.

Quantum physics is the science that explains how everything in the universe came into being and works. It is the study of why, what and how the universe and everything therein, exists. This is done by breaking down 'stuff' into its most basic components.

As you will see, all things are intricately interlinked: spirituality, thoughts, emotions, beliefs, physical matter, the world, the universe and so on. Interconnected and interwoven in much the same way as the spider weaves its web, each strand connecting with another may not directly link in with one strand, but is still connected via other strands to the whole.

Quantum physics is exciting and, although complex, it can be broken down, which is what quantum physics itself does, into smaller, more digestible pieces.

Most of us would have learned at school that matter - you, me, the table, the television and the computer I am diligently working on at this moment - is made up of tiny molecules. These molecules can be broken down further into atoms. Atoms can be further broken down into sub-atomic particles which consist of photons, electrons, neutrons, leptons and so forth. Atoms that vibrate at the same frequency are drawn together to form matter. This is 'like attracts like' operating at the micro level.

It was Isaac Newton who theorised that the universe was made up of solid objects, atoms which were held together by gravity. Newton believed that atoms were solid in nature.

Now, in the early part of the 20th Century, Albert Einstein made a groundbreaking discovery that was to turn Newtonian physics on its head. What Albert Einstein discovered was that atoms were made up of sub-atomic particles which appeared solid, but were, in actual fact, pure energy. The equation for this became known as $E=MC^2$. It is now known that gravity does not hold together the particles that make up the atom. If this were so the natural course of action of the electron, which moves around the nucleus, would be that it would radiate away its energy and the electron would spiral into the nucleus. It would in effect collapse. This would mean that everything in the universe including you and me would collapse.

Here's the gist of $E=MC^2$. All matter is 99.9999999% empty space and when broken down into the most basic components it is made up of the same stuff. And this stuff is called energy.

If matter (an object with mass) is 99.9999999% empty space, why does it appear to be solid? Why does the empty space that we call our body not pass through the other empty space we call a wall? This is because the speed at which electrons spin around the nucleus of the matter which makes up our bodies creates a wall or barrier. If you think of a ceiling fan, when it is turned off you can pass your hand in between the stationary blades. Turn the fan on and it becomes impossible to pass your hand through because the blades create a kind of barrier. In much the same way, when one atom comes in contact with another the orbiting electrons prevent them from passing through one another and they act as if they were solid objects.

This is exciting. Everything that exists in the universe whether you can see it or not, including colour, sound waves, the page you are reading, your desk, bed, floor, garden, dog, cat, sense of smell, are all made up of 99.9999999% empty space. Wow!

It was to be a man named Neils Bohr, who was to give another twist to Einstein's theory. He claimed that the sub-atomic particles weren't actually particles, but existed as waves of energy. Einstein and Bohr debated this for many years. As it turns out they were both quite correct.

As technology advanced it became possible, don't ask me how, for scientists to perform experiments on these sub-atomic particles/waves. Here's what they discovered. The sub-atomic particles/waves behave according to the belief of the scientist doing the experiment. In other words, a particle can either behave as a wave of energy or a particle, depending on what the scientist believes it will do. Further, if the scientist changes his mind about what he believes it will do then the particle will change in accordance with his expectation.

Here's another thing that is of interest. A particle, let's say an electron for example, can tunnel through solid objects. This has been called 'quantum tunnelling'. If for instance you were to place an electron into a container that does not contain any holes or 'tunnels', the electron will 'tunnel' outside the glass. The electron does not actually 'move' outside of the container, it just appears outside instantaneously. If it sounds weird, that's because it is weird!

There was another very famous scientist, Erwin Schrodinger, who discovered what was to be called Quantum Entanglement. What this basically means is that if a particle is split in two, and the two halves are separated by any amount of distance, they will communicate with each other with complete disregard for the time and space that separates them. Communication between the two happens in zero time. What this means is that energy does not travel. It just *is*. Instantly.

In one experiment conducted by the US Army a sample of DNA was taken from a man's mouth and moved over a thousand kilometres away. The man was then given disturbing visual images to watch on a screen. What they discovered was the DNA responded to the emotional reaction elicited by the images at *exactly* the precise moment that the images were viewed by the man. There was no time delay. The distance of separation and time between the man and his DNA was irrelevant.

If your head is now spinning, here's a rundown to simplify:

- Atoms are made up of sub-atomic particles.
- Particles, atoms and matter are 99.9999999% empty space.
- Matter appears solid because of the speed at which the electrons, protons etc spin around the nucleus of the atom.
- Particles may behave like a wave of energy and/or a particle (solid).
- The expectation of the person watching the particle/wave/energy determines its behaviour.
- All particles, and therefore matter, are made up of energy.
- Matter cannot be created or destroyed; it can only change its form.
- All things within the universe are made up of this vibrating energy.
- Atoms are attracted to other atoms that are vibrating at a similar frequency.
- Particles, the smallest part of an atom, can perform amazing feats of Quantum Tunnelling through solid objects.

- Energy communicates instantly, with complete disregard for space and time.

So this is quantum physics in a nutshell. Let's have a look now at another interesting finding.

THIN PLACES

Heaven and earth are three feet apart,
but within the thin places this distance is
even smaller...

Celtic Saying

In Celtic tradition, sacred spiritual places exist within our landscape known as 'thin places' where the veil between the living and the dead, between heaven and earth, is very fine. Thin places restore, revitalise and refresh our spirit, soul and heart and often abound with nature's spirits. Mountains, lakes, rivers, caves, and the sea are all examples of thin places.

Make plans to spend some time in a 'thin place'. If you live in a city you might like to consider getting out of town for a few days. If this is not possible then even just an early morning trip to a park or local public gardens or the beach can be soulful. Take time to contemplate, meditate, pray or simply connect with the 'spirit of place' that is present. Get to know it, feel it and be at one with it.

Write in your journal about what you saw, heard, felt or sensed whilst spending time in this 'thin place'.

Twelve

THE G SPOT

I don't believe in an afterlife, although I am bringing a change of underwear...

Woody Allen

I n 1997, at the University of California in San Diego, a group of neuroscientists discovered that people with epilepsy, who have a particular type of brain seizure, are known to become much more spiritually oriented, have visions of a profound spiritual nature and are generally much more in touch with their God. People who have these types of seizures typically report having frequent intense spiritual experiences, leading scientists to believe that the brain may well be hard-wired to produce such experiences.

Whilst studying this group of people it was found that an area of the temporal lobe had much higher measurements of electrical activity created during seizures. This was also found to be the case if they simply thought about God or spiritual concepts. Scientists believe these experiences were created by over-stimulation of the temporal lobe during the epileptic seizures. They have called this part of the brain the God Module or God Spot.

Since the time of these experiments it has been discovered that it is primarily the medial right temporal lobe, together with the hippocampus and other limbic lobe areas, to be specific, that are involved in the mediation of spiritual experiences. I will refer here only to the temporal lobe and associated areas for easier reading.

There are drugs that can stimulate the temporal lobe into producing a spiritual experience. In one study Psilocybin, an extract from hallucinogenic mushrooms, was given to volunteers. Of the 36 people involved in the experiment more than 60% described having full blown spiritual experiences according to psychological scales. Two-thirds reported that it was the most spiritually significant event in their lives or rated it in the top five (data taken from *News in Science – Magic Mushrooms Hit the God Spot)*. It is believed that this drug stimulated the medial temporal lobes, and associated areas, creating a spiritual experience.

Professor David Nichols from Purdue University School of Pharmacy commented that the same neurological processes are triggered when using the drug Psilocybin as when we fast, meditate or have a near-death experience. He further states that research in this field, known as neurotheology, could bring about understanding of the 'molecular alterations in the brain that underlie religious and mystical experiences'.

In his book, *What Happens When We Die*, Dr Sam Parnia poses the hypothesis that the brain 'mediates' near-death experiences. He states that this does not tell us whether these experiences are real or not real, but 'they may be very significant in that they may help to discover new ways to manipulate the brain and mediate the same effect as an NDE (near-death experience)'. He goes on to say, 'People who suffer with depressive tendencies, for example, may benefit from artificial activation of the same areas of the brain that mediate NDEs.'

It would seem to be fairly accurate to suggest that most near-death experiences are life-changing events. Many people report that as a result of their near-death experience they are no longer afraid of death, are much less materialistic, more spiritual and less worried in general. It would seem to be a life-enhancing event to many who have this experience, causing long-term changes in the way they live their lives. This, as Dr Parnia concludes, leads to 'long-term brain-based changes in the body'. It would appear that the near-death experience changes our neurology.

Hold on to your judgments now because I'd like you to meet David, for whom taking Ecstasy produced two near-death experiences that were to change his life. When David first contacted me I thought, perhaps like many of you are thinking now, no I don't think it is the same thing as a spontaneous near-death experience. But perhaps it *is* just the other side of the same coin.

DAVID'S STORY

My experience was substance induced, but I would say that although the drug acted as a catalyst to aid me to enter this realm, looking back, I think it was a combination of timing, people, place and my fairly long history of deep enquiry into my inner nature. I do not think it would have happened just by taking Ecstasy alone. I was ready to have this experience even if I had no clue as to what was about to happen. Some people devalue experiences like mine because of the dreaded word 'drugs'. But what's the difference between a heart attack, a near brush with death in some way or a drug? They are all catalysts.

It was in the mid eighties and I was living in Hobart, Tasmania, where I was working as a rebirther, running workshops, training groups and doing individual sessions. I had a close group of friends including my partner who became interested in taking Ecstasy. Ecstasy was a new phenomenon and was not illegal at this stage.

One day we agreed to gather at my house, we meditated around a table and then took our dose. Sometime later, a few of the group said they were going for a walk, but I decided to stay back. As the substance began to take effect I sat down on a chair and began to fall into a deep meditative state. This happened quite spontaneously and I felt myself sinking ever inward and I remember marvelling at how deeply I could travel inside. It was as if a space was opening up all the time.

I became aware of the others returning from their walk. My partner looked at me and I heard her say, 'We have to move him to a better part of the house.' Once moved my partner said to me, 'Look into my eyes,' and as I did this my eyes started quivering. I then became aware of my eyes rolling upwards into my eye sockets.

Then I died!!!

I felt this dying process so clearly, it was ecstatic. There was this extraordinary feeling of release, and I experienced a sloughing off of unwanted, no longer needed parts of myself, parts that weren't relevant that had been hanging on to my soul like dead leaves – parts that had been there so long I had lost awareness of them. I heard myself saying out loud to the others, who by now had gathered around me, 'It's so good to die.' Suddenly I found myself in this infinite black void. No tunnel of light or anything like that, just an instant shift into this timeless black void. I was very aware of everything and what struck me first was this sense of no time, no past, no future. Just eternal now.

In the distance I became aware of this gigantic structure floating out there in the timeless void. I saw it had portals out of which I saw lines of golden light. On the lines of light I could see movement back and forth. From the distance they looked like little corpuscles of gold and I knew that those little blobs were human souls. They travelled out and in and I sensed a feeling of enormous power and purpose. I couldn't see where these lines of light were stretching to. Later my words for describing this amazing place was 'Cosmic Grand Central'.

Then a new awareness came over me: I know this place! It was like a buried memory stirring out of somewhere. This is where I go to at the end of every life. I return here. I did not recall what went on here after dying and I didn't go into the place either. But the returning memory of this place was an enormous gift for me.

A day or two later David was to re-enter the Cosmic Grand Central once again.

He states:

I felt I was being sucked out of my body. I yelled, 'I'm going again.' I was in the same inky, black, timeless void. I was looking back at the structure which I called Cosmic Grand Central and I recall thinking to myself, This is amazing to go to a place like this twice. Then I found myself on one of those golden pathways which I had seen in the distance a few days before. Now I was on it! It was large and must have been made of pure golden light. It was slanting upwards towards some divine destination. I travelled upwards, aware that I was carrying my life experiences to date with me (I was in my forties at this time). The sense of carrying my life experiences was very important – I guess it's what you do take with you, your true possessions. I was travelling upwards at quite a pace and feeling this enormous state of exultation, a feeling that I had never had before in my life. I travelled up and up on this golden highway and I became aware of this gigantic, intelligent universe. I saw that God was everything and so beyond all human concepts, and I felt this feeling of unity with this gigantic intelligence. I was a part of it and myself at the same time. I was God and I was my human self. I was the ocean and remained the drop of water. It was such a powerful realisation that somehow can only be seen in that higher dimension.

So, this is the story that changed my life forever.

David goes on to say:

For so many years I searched for the truth of that part of me which so many books said survived death of the physical body. It was not enough for me to just read about it. I wanted experiential facts. I wanted to KNOW. After that journey out of the physical I KNEW!

For a long time I didn't want to talk about it. I held back because it is, to me, so sacred and is not to be spilled out all over the place at random. I didn't want it misunderstood or desecrated by the doubts and judgments that other people can have. I just couldn't do that, it was too dear to me. It's much easier for me to talk about it now, if the need arises. So from time to time, I share the story with someone and when I do the timing is always right.

It took months of reflection to integrate this experience into my life. It left me with a profound feeling of peace and happiness. It changed my energy and how I related to people. When discussing the vicissitudes of life I feel a sense of 'knowing' which brings me new ways of approaching problems that people always have from time to time. What I had was an enlightening experience and it changed my whole self forever after. I don't claim to be enlightened; I am still very human and happy with that.

Whilst I would like to state that using drugs to induce any mystical experience is not endorsed by the author in any way, as I re-read what David has written I am struck by the sheer honesty and frankness with which he shares his story. I also am aware of the similarities between this experience and the one encountered by Jacqueline, whom we met earlier in Chapter Seven.

This does make me wonder if perhaps there may be a place for controlled drug-induced spiritual experiences in people with mental issues such as severe lifelong depression. It certainly is thought provoking.

NURTURE YOURSELF

Nurturing yourself is important at any time in your life. Often we get so busy with the 'stuff' of life that we forget to take time out to simply look after ourselves. You are just as important as anyone else on this planet and will function better if you take the time to look after yourself.

Ask yourself this: how often do I take time out to do something nice just for myself? When was the last time? If you can't remember then you definitely need to do this exercise.

Make a list of things you'd really like to do and pick one. Make a commitment to do this one activity within the next 24 hours. You can pick more than one providing you are willing to commit to doing them. Here are some ideas to get you going.

- Go to your favourite bookshop and spend an afternoon browsing the books you love. Select one or two that take your fancy and purchase them. Do it without guilt! Make a decision to just enjoy the moment.

- Alternatively go for an early morning walk, either on a beach or in the bush, somewhere that connects you with nature, and breathe in the fresh air, and really experience it. Notice ten things on your walk that are beautiful and touch you in some way. It could be the smell of the air, a leaf, the colour of a flower, a cloud formation.

- Arrange to have coffee with a dear friend. Let them know how much you enjoy their company.

- Join a yoga class. Or have a bubble bath. Have a massage. Go to a day spa and have 'the works'.

Record your experience in your journal.

Make a commitment to do this on a regular basis. Schedule it into your week.

Thirteen

THE DOORWAY

*Unless you know what it is, I ain't never going to be able
to explain it to you...*

Louis Armstrong (talking about jazz)

As we have seen, it appears that when the temporal lobe is stimulated it allows the brain to mediate phenomena of a highly spiritual nature. I use the word 'mediate' because I do not believe that the brain 'creates', but rather acts to facilitate these experiences.

Stimulation of these areas in the brain is like knocking on a door. The experience we have, whether it be a near-death experience, nearing-death awareness or after-death communication, naturally occurs once the doorway has been opened.

Taking this further, when we die we not only step through the doorway, but close it firmly behind us. This doorway, however, is not locked, merely closed.

Using the above analogy, it appears that there are many ways to knock on the doorway of the temporal lobe. As we have seen, drugs and seizures are both ways, although rather dramatic not to mention unhealthy, of tapping into these experiences. But there are other ways to stimulate the temporal lobe.

Most, but not all, near-death experiences happen when there is extreme trauma to the body, when it is either about to die or is already clinically dead with no electrical signals present in the brain. Some near-death experiences happen when death is perceived as highly likely, but has not yet actually caused any physical trauma to the body. The trauma, whether it is perceived or actual, creates physical, emotional, mental and spiritual stress within the body and brain.

People who have deathbed visions or nearing-death awareness are also undergoing stress of a physical, emotional, mental and indeed spiritual nature. However, as they move closer to death it is not uncommon for family members to comment that they seem more lucid, more aware and more at peace. Perhaps this is in part due to the impact of deathbed visions, or awareness of other things that are outside of their normal range of awareness. This sense of peacefulness is also often present in the near-death experience.

People who are bereaved or are waiting for a loved one to die are also, in many cases, experiencing extreme multi-layered levels of stress. This is a most difficult time.

So there is a common thread, something linking all of these experiences: intense physical, emotional, mental and spiritual stress, which leads to the spiritual phenomena we call near-death experience, near-death awareness and after-death communication which, in turn, leads to equally intense feelings of peacefulness.

In a nutshell, the brain is undergoing changes. It is functioning outside its normal modus operandi. Chemicals are whizzing around and areas of the brain that may not usually be fully utilised are going full steam ahead. Other areas of the brain may close down or stop functioning during these times. I believe that the stress caused during these times, albeit out of our control, is stimulating the temporal lobe and associated areas, allowing perception of highly spiritual phenomena to occur.

Other ways to stimulate the temporal lobe may include meditation, hypnosis, praying or doing anything that is spiritually uplifting, causing us to 'flex' this area of the brain. This seems like a contradiction in terms, a paradox, as the relaxation required for hypnosis, meditation, prayer and so forth is just the opposite to extreme emotional, physical and mental stress. However, these activities do invoke spiritual experiences and are generally much healthier in nature. They allow us to open the doorway of the right temporal lobe, to alter consciousness, without the stress of being engaged in physical trauma of any kind.

So what happens once we step through the spiritual doorway of the right temporal lobe and associated areas? What happens once this area of the brain is actively stimulated either via physical, emotional, mental and spiritual trauma or by meditation or hypnosis?

I believe that the opening of the doorway is where we cross the threshold and step into spiritual realms. This seems to be where the 'funny stuff' starts to happen. And it is at this point that consciousness and the brain/body seem to separate. Consciousness or spirit appears to be able to move outside of the body and exist independently of the physical body.

Once the doorway is open it is then that consciousness can and does begin to be aware of other realities that are normally outside of our awareness. If we are about to die or experience physical trauma to our body then we may have what has been termed a near-death experience. We may begin to move outside our body, to view it from the vantage point of floating above, move along a dark tunnel into bright light and so forth. Here we may be aware of our family members and friends who have already died or other spiritual beings. It's like we have one foot on each side of the doorway.

Electrical signals in the brain are not essential for consciousness to move outside the doorway (the body). This is why the near-death experiences are reported during the time of flat lining, when the brain is clinically dead and is not capable of coherent thoughts or the laying down of memory.

In the case of bereavement, although we may not directly experience physical trauma to our body as a result of the loss, we are most certainly 'traumatised' emotionally, mentally and spiritually, and it is this trauma that enables our brain to expand our awareness so we may see, sense, hear, smell or feel the touch of the person who has died. It is here that we may also 'dream' about our loved ones. As previously stated dreams are often of a very different quality and may incorporate all of our senses. Our brain is open and receptive to the input.

It is not uncommon, however, for a person who is bereaved to endure some physical symptoms as a direct result of the loss. The exact reasons for this are largely still unknown, but it may be due to a lowering of immune system functioning which creates stress on the entire body. Family members may experience pain in an area of their body where their loved one was injured. For example, in the case of a cardiac arrest resulting in death, cardiac symptoms may be experienced in the living partner. This can continue to be problematic at anniversaries and on special occasions for many years and is a well documented phenomenon.

FAY'S STORY

Twelve months after my brother-in-law, John, died, my husband, Ken, and I drove to Armidale to visit Beth, my husband's sister. John had held a prominent position within the university so we watched a DVD of him receiving an award. Then, turning the TV onto the news, Beth and my husband left the room. I was sitting by myself when the hair stood up on my arms. I could feel a closeness to me. I turned around and there was John, looking straight at my face. I must have jumped a foot off my chair. My husband walked back in and John just disappeared. I asked Beth did she feel John was in the house. She said no, but the group he used to go walking with said they often heard his footsteps walking with them.

So what does our understanding of the God spot, the quantum world and levels of consciousness say about Fay's experience? What does it say about John? These are not easy questions to answer, and of course are subject to debate. What does it say about what happens when we die?

Firstly, Fay has just watched a DVD of John so she is probably relaxed, tuned in to John, absorbed in what she is doing. This means that her brain wave frequencies have altered and she has entered a light trance. Her brain has tuned in and is open and ready to receive. If we were to measure Fay's brain frequencies we would probably find that they had slowed to the Alpha range of around 7 to 14 cycles per second. Fay would be totally unaware that this had happened, but she might feel relaxed or she might be internally focused on the memories of her brother-in-law. Either way at some point she has slipped into Alpha state. The action of slowing down the brain frequencies has just called into action other parts of Fay's brain, namely her unconscious mind.

It is likely that the God spot, the right temporal lobe and associated limbic areas of Fay's brain, is stimulated maybe because of a number of factors including being relaxed, internally focused on memories of John, emotions associated with those memories and so forth. Fay also goes on to report that this was not an isolated incident, that she has had many other similar experiences throughout her life. So Fay's mind is quite adept at tuning in this way.

Now, what about John? Where is he?

Because everything is made up of the same energy, it follows that consciousness or spirit is also pure energy. There is simply nothing else. Energy cannot be created or destroyed but merely changes its form. What more do I need to say here? John has not gone anywhere, he's right there in the room.

TRACEY'S STORY

Swiftly I drove along the dark highway, my headlights piercing light through blackness as ghostly images of gum trees glided silently by. My mother was dying and I wanted to be with her. Suddenly I saw my mother. She was not the alert, good-looking and interested 90 year old she'd been a month or so earlier, but a very beautiful, ecstatically happy 23 year old. She smiled radiantly at me for a number of seconds and then disappeared.

I knew she had died.

I left the highway at the next exit to phone my brother. Emotionally and yet gladly he said, 'No need to hurry, she's gone.'

I later learned that our mother had also appeared to our eldest brother who was in a plane speeding from New Guinea, so he too realised that she had just died. One of our nephews reached the front porch of the nursing home as my mother appeared to him. He too realised that she had just died. The image our mother presented to me was identical with that seen by my brother and my nephew.

Inside the nursing home our mother was happily surrounded by most of her family as she moved on to the next stage of her adventures.

In this beautiful story Tracey's mum appears in several places at the same time in order to let her family members know that she has died. This illustrates well the quantum idea that consciousness and spirit, which is pure energy, does not 'move' but simply 'is', with complete disregard for space and time. It 'is', instantaneously.

If space and time existed within the realms of spirit then of course it would be impossible for Tracey's mother to appear to the three of them at roughly the same time.

It would seem that when the 'matter' that is our bodies begins to die, or at certain critical times in our lives, it 'frees' up consciousness, via stimulation of the right temporal lobe and associated areas of the brain, which appears to allow us to be aware of and tune into things that are not normally in our range of sensing.

Everything in the universe as we know it, including you and me, vibrates. Increase the speed at which matter vibrates and it naturally begins to change its form. Remember matter cannot be created or destroyed, it merely changes its form. Take water for example. The particles that make up the water vibrate at a particular frequency. This gives water the appearance of being solid. When you put your hand into the water it gets wet. Now let's make the particles that make up the water vibrate faster. We do this by heating the water up. When you heat a substance the particles move faster. Basic chemistry. Okay, so we boil the water. Make the particles vibrate faster and what happens? The matter that is the water is no longer solid. It has changed its form. If you pass your hand through it now, it will most definitely feel different to what it did when it was wet and sitting in the bowl. In fact your hand will pass right through it. It is no longer a 'solid' - water - the particles are now vibrating so fast it is now steam. Matter, our bodies for example, appears solid because we are vibrating at a slow frequency. Consciousness on the other hand is pure energy and as such vibrates at a very fast rate.

Particles are attracted to other particles that are vibrating at a similar frequency, which is why many people who are nearing death see family members who have already died. It's as though they have just climbed aboard the same train. In other words, we begin to vibrate at a similar frequency to, and so become more aware of, another reality - a reality where our deceased loved ones are visible and able to communicate with us and vice versa.

According to the *Macquarie Dictionary,* consciousness, spirit and soul are defined in this way:

Consciousness
1. a state of being conscious. 2. inward sensibility of something; knowledge of one's own existence, sensations, cognitions etc. 3. the thoughts and feelings, collectively, of an individual or of an aggregate of people: the moral consciousness of a nation. 4. activity of mental faculties: to regain consciousness after fainting. 5. raise one's consciousness, to raise the level of one's understanding and sensitivity to cultural and social issues.

Spirit
1. The principle of conscious life, originally identified with the breath; the vital principle in man, animating the body or mediating between body and soul. 2. The incorporeal part of man: present in spirit though absent in body.

3. The soul as separable from the body at death. 4. Conscious, incorporeal being, as opposed to matter: the world of spirit.

Soul
1. The principle of life, feeling, thought and action in man, regarded as a distinct entity separate from the body, and commonly held to be separable in existence from the body; the spiritual part of man as distinct from the physical. 2. the spiritual part of man regarded in its moral aspect, or as believed to survive death and be subject to happiness or misery in a life to come. 3. A disembodied spirit of a deceased person.

As you can clearly see, there are degrees of difference between consciousness, spirit and soul. I think perhaps that spirit and soul are one and the same, and it is the spirit or soul that maintains consciousness after bodily death. I suspect that spirit or soul and consciousness are inseparable.

Consciousness, it seems, is about being more aware, more conscious. This is the paradox then, because our awareness of virtually all nearing-death awareness, near-death experiences, after-death communications occur during states of altered consciousness or when the brain is highly active in the limbic regions, the subconscious mind.

The soul, spirit or consciousness does not evaporate into nothing. It is here with you all the time. There is no separation. There is no death in the doom and gloom way in which it has been portrayed for so long. Death, rather like the speeding electron whizzing around the nucleus creating the illusion of solidity, is just that – an illusion. And at odd moments in our lives we get snippets, tantalising glimpses, we see the reality of what is. We become more 'conscious' of what is.

It would appear that when the physical body dies, all the memories and thoughts and love remain. Consciousness, spirit or soul it would seem, remains intact.

Some people experience spontaneous contact with their loved ones irrespective of their beliefs in an afterlife. Indeed in my research for this book I have spoken to many people who have said they did not 'believe in any of this stuff' - until it happened to them. This spontaneous contact can happen at various times throughout life, sometimes just after a loved one has died and sometimes many years later. A personal crisis may induce such a contact. But it is just as likely to happen whilst tending to a mundane task. Sleep also seems to be a particularly favourable environment for such events.

The relationship you have held with your loved one does not suddenly cease to exist because of death. The truth is that love between two souls is eternal, providing an opportunity to enter into a new relationship with your loved one. It may not be what you had planned, but life takes you on many twists and turns along the way. Be gentle with yourself. Finding a place of acceptance may never come. Not finding a place of acceptance may be unbearable. It would appear that people who have experienced contact with their loved one in some way find their place of peace more easily. It is comforting to 'know', and let me tell you, once you have had an experience you do 'know' - beyond any shadow of doubt.

Robbin Renee Bridges, author of *A Bridge of Love Between Heaven & Earth,* poses the theory that this energy that is our spirit is still right here with us. There is nowhere it 'goes' to but here. She states, 'The realms of light (heaven) surround and enfold this physical world. We are unaware of the next world in the same way that a foetus is unaware of the world outside the mother's womb.'

I like this. I do not think there is anywhere else to go. There is no place called heaven or hell. Our loved ones are here all the time. They never leave. Separation is an illusion. At certain times during our lives, more commonly when we are grieving or moving towards death ourselves, which creates emotional, physical, mental and spiritual stress on the body and brain, we are able to perceive what we usually cannot. The trauma stimulates a part of our brain that mediates such experiences so we are able to be aware of them.

Similarly when we meditate, or use hypnosis we are providing our brain with fertile, rich ground in which to perceive such encounters.

Consciousness travels instantaneously, and in no time. Our loved ones are here all the time. All you have to do is be open and ready to communicate with them, and here they are. The truth is we can all do this, because we are hard wired to do so.

And I'm about to show you how.

Part 4

THE RAINBOW

The energy of spirits vibrates at a very high rate, while ours goes much slower because we are in physical bodies. How we bridge the gap dictates how well communications traverse these two dimensions...

One Last Time

John Edward

FOUND

The boy sat near the camp fire that he had lit. Evening was descending and the stars were like pinpricks on a black canvas, letting light through from far away.

He had left his hut many months ago now, and he had travelled a lot. He had seen places he never thought he would. He had met with some interesting travellers along the way. Some had listened with their hearts to his stories. Others had laughed them away, blind in their hearts and deaf in their souls. But the boy did not care. He had a story to tell regardless of whether he was believed or not.

But, for the first time in a while, something stirred inside him. A yearning for something he could not really explain. He felt restless and he was not sure why.

His mind could not concentrate on anything, flying from thought to thought. As he was preparing to bed down for the night he thought about the old lady. He wished he could find her, find the other people from that special night. He would love to be sitting near that fire again, blind in the eyes but alert in his heart.

He had tried walking back to where that evening took place, but he must have been lost because he never found that wall again. Yet he felt certain that he was in the right place. But the wall was not there anymore, almost as if it had never existed. With these thoughts in his mind he went to sleep.

'Boy, wake up.' The soft voice hardly registered in his sleep. 'Wake up, it's time.' The voice became louder and had firmness in its tone. The boy turned towards the sound, slowly opening his eyes to adjust to the semi darkness. He felt confused, caught in that altered state between sleep and wake. Bringing his torso upright he looked to his right and saw the old lady. It was as if she had always been there, sitting quietly near what remained of his camp fire.

She looked at him gently with patience in her eyes. The boy tried to sit up, but her hand gently pushed him back down on the ground. 'No, do not move. Lie down and relax,' she said as she reached for something by her side. The boy noticed that she was holding his wooden bowl, careful so as not to spill its content. 'Drink boy,' she said as she gently placed the bowl to his lips. 'Drink and close your eyes.'

This is definitely a strange dream, the boy thought as he drank from the bowl, *and it feels so real*. When he had drunk all the contents of the bowl, the lady urged him to close his eyes once more. The boy's head felt light, just like once before at his village, when as a little boy he drank some of the fermented juice meant for special celebrations. Memories were coming back quickly now.

'It feels funny,' he said in a whisper. 'I feel like everything around me is moving.'

'Maybe it is, maybe it isn't,' the old lady replied. 'Maybe it is you who are moving. There are many different kinds of journeys. Journeys of the body, journeys of the mind and journeys of the soul.' She gently stroked his forehead and the boy thought about his grandmother. She also used to pass her hand in his hair when he was falling asleep. And the thought brought tears to his eyes.

'You have already come so far from your little hut,' she continued, and there was something magical in her voice. He felt transported far away to other times. 'But there is one final journey you must take. I will be there with you. I will follow wherever you go and you will always be safe.'

The boy did not doubt that, and he found himself standing on a hill looking down on his old village.

The old lady's voice brought him back to her. As if reading his mind she answered his unspoken question, 'It is your village, look closer.' Her hand swept in front of his face and he felt all the images become sharper, clearer. 'Look with your soul, not with your eyes. Your eyes may trick you, but your soul will never lie to you.'

The boy kept his eyes on the village below, and he could not believe what he saw. *I am really dreaming then*, he thought aloud, *because it is not possible that I can see them.* Tears freely flowing down his cheeks now.

The old lady held his hand, 'Yes, it is your parents that you are seeing. Do not be afraid now.' She squeezed his hand harder to give him comfort. 'You can always choose - life is full of choices. If you want, you can walk down the hill and meet half way with them, or you can just stay here and look from afar.'

The boy did not know what to do. *I am just having a dream,* he repeated to himself. *This is not real,* he reassured himself. Whilst he was a bit afraid of these strange events, he felt a longing to be there with his parents. To see them once more, and to reconnect.

'I want to go,' he said aloud and with conviction, and started to take a step forward.

The old lady gently held him back and said, 'I will go first. I will show you the way, just follow my voice.' And the lady led the way down the hill, the boy a few steps behind, following her voice deeper and deeper into the valley.

Once at the bottom of the hill, and a short walk away from the village, the lady stopped and with a piece of wood collected nearby, drew a circle around the boy. 'Just stay in this circle, and allow them to come to you. I am sure that there are things that need to be said between you.' And the old lady took a few steps away. 'A sacred exchange between souls that belong to each other. I need not be here, but remember that my voice will stay with you.' She took a few more steps away as she talked, 'Listen with your heart and say everything that needs to be said, do not be afraid. If you ever want to talk with me again, just close your eyes and speak from your soul. I will listen. But I think that I have served my purpose now.'

And with that she walked away, leaving a young boy in a circle drawn in the sand. A boy with closed eyes and an open heart.

Fourteen

DARKNESS

Adam gently touched her on the forehead with a long finger.
'It's all inside there, Jane, like a box with many compartments.
Each one you can call upon for anything you want or desire. It
contains the greatest magic of all.'

The Man Who Was Magic

Paul Gallico

R e-connecting after loss, as we have seen, often happens quite spontaneously. These experiences are quite normal and natural, we are hardwired to have them. But what if it doesn't happen spontaneously? Does that mean your loved one did not love you? Does that mean that you cannot do it? Does that mean that they are lost forever? You know in your heart and soul that it does not.

In this part of the book we will explore how you can create that link intentionally and activate the infinite wisdom that is within you to engage in a meaningful and healing relationship with your loved one. We assume that once someone has died that it is final, the door is closed and they are gone forever. This is our perspective. But it would seem that for our loved ones who have died it is a given that the relationship continues. Often the moment that we give ourselves 'space' to receive, either via meditation, hypnosis or dreams or some other form of altered state of awareness, there they are, ready and waiting and willing to come to the party.

There is a beautiful story that I have told elsewhere for different reasons, the origins of which escape me, but I will relate it here for you as it illustrates a point beautifully.

Once upon a time, in a far away village, an old woman was searching for something outside her house. She was on her knees diligently running her hands in the soil and grass. Someone saw her and asked, 'What are you looking for?'

'I am searching for a ring,' the old woman replied.

'Then I will help you look,' said the passer-by. And some other people who were passing saw and also stopped to help look for the elusive ring. But, search as they might, no-one could find the ring.

A young boy, who had also stopped to help the woman in her quest, asked wisely, 'Where did you lose this ring?'

The woman replied, 'I lost it inside the house, young man.'

A bit surprised the young fellow asked, 'Then why are you searching out here in the garden?'

And the old woman looked up at the young boy and spoke, 'Because inside it is dark.'

This is so true. We think we have lost someone and our heart is broken. We look at the vacant chair where she used to sit, hoping she's there. But she is not. We visit a much favoured beach where we used to stroll hand in hand, but we do it alone. We lay in bed, with hopes of just one last good night kiss that never comes. We stew on what we have lost, what is no longer. And each time we do this we are looking, like the old lady in the story, outside of ourselves, when what we seek lies within. Inside, as in the story, it may well be dark territory. But only by going within ourselves can we unlock the magic that is ours for the keeping.

Let's have a look, now, at how we can begin to look inside that darkness within ourselves. Let's flood it with colour and light and allow this to reach out across time and space, to flow from your heart to theirs, in a blaze of light - a rainbow of connection.

A word of caution before we begin. Spontaneous contact may happen at any moment with or without facilitation. The techniques in this part of the book are specifically designed to allow you to engage in after-death communication. These experiences will probably feel very real. If you feel uncomfortable at any time with the exercises outlined, then I would like you to respect your feelings and stop and wait a while, this may simply not be the right time. Be gentle with yourself, take your time. There is no rush. Your loved one will be there when the time is right for you.

PERCHANCE To DREAM

Sleep is an excellent vehicle for communication with your loved one. There is a very different quality to 'dreams' of this nature. They are more than just dreams. They have a feeling of reality about them and may include senses such as sight, sounds, smells, tactile sensations and are often accompanied by intense emotions, feelings of love, peace, understanding, forgiveness and so forth. Think of these as 'contacts' or 'communications' rather than just dreams.

If dream recall is difficult for you, keep this in mind: these dreams are not dreams, they are visitations. You do not need to have excellent dream recall in order to remember a visitation. After death communication almost exclusively happens not during the dream phase of sleep, known as REM (rapid eye movement), but just after falling asleep or upon wakening. This is not a dream. It is irrelevant if you have difficulty remembering dreams.

Here's how to foster contact through sleep:

- Keep a small journal at the side of your bed to record your experiences as soon as possible after they have happened.

- Each night when you go to sleep talk to your loved one, invite them to make contact with you. Let them know that you are willing and waiting to communicate with them. This can be as easy as a short prayer or you can simply say, 'Jo, I would really love for you to visit me, please come and be with me. I love you and I want to talk with you, to know you are okay. I am opening myself up to being with you.'

- At first it is quite normal to only get snippets, like I did with my dad. Small, little bits of conversations. You might only hear words, the sound of your loved one's voice, or perhaps only the scent of your loved one's perfume. Perhaps you will be able to see them, but not hear them. This is normal. Just keep on asking, keep on inviting them in. It will happen eventually.

- Sleeping with an item of clothing, cuddling up to a much loved jumper or shirt may also help your mind to open up to contact. The feeling of the item of clothing or perhaps the smell or the familiarity of it may help to open the line of communication. It helps to create a link and is something that is familiar to both of you.

- If your loved one visits you during sleep and you don't understand the message they are trying to convey, check with your feelings. When they contacted you what did you *feel.* Sometimes our feelings convey more than words. If you still can't understand, don't worry. Just record the experience in your journal. In your mind, just let your loved one know that you didn't quite understand and they will keep trying until you get the message.

- If you really are not quite getting the message, but the 'dreams' are coming thick and fast then try asking yourself this: *If my loved one was trying to give me a message, what would it be?* Turn this question over in your mind, listen for the answer and write it down.

- Record anything you feel is relevant in your journal as soon as you wake up. Recording your special communications in this way allows you to observe similarities and connections between visitations. It also allows you to remember exactly what was said and what took place. There is nothing worse than not being able to remember what words have been spoken. You will always remember the event, the feelings associated with the contact, but sometimes over time the exact words are forgotten. Write it down.

- Remember the three Ps. Be **Prepared** for contact – it feels very real when it happens. Be **Patient** – it may take time. And be **Persistent**.

Fifteen

CONNECTIONS

'There are compartments just for that called "I can" and "I will".
When you have learned to unlock them, the strong magic will
help you to move mountains.'

The Man Who Was Magic

Paul Gallico

L et's face it. When someone you love dies there is almost nothing you wouldn't give to have just one more chance, another opportunity to hold them, to simply be with them.

You think about what you should have said, what you could have said. Maybe you didn't get to say goodbye. Perhaps there were unspoken things that you would give anything to be able to say. And what about the words *I love you*? All these may sound trivial, small things, perhaps we said them every day without thought. Perhaps we never said them at all. But when someone we love has died it can be unbearable if we didn't get to say *I love you* just one more time. Or what about, *I'm sorry* – one of the hardest things is when someone we love dies just after an argument. Maybe you said something unkind, maybe they did. Maybe you just want to know that they are okay. Perhaps there is a need to 'chat' on a daily basis, to tap into their wisdom, to ask and receive answers to life's trials and tribulations.

I know when my dad died I couldn't believe that he had just gone and I didn't get to say goodbye. I would have done anything to be able to have just one last goodbye. The last time we spoke was the night before he died. It was all trivial stuff. Having taken their little dog, Muffin, to the vet he lamented how expensive it was, costing $100 for a small dog to have one injection. I laughed and said, 'Dad, you're a bit out of touch.' He laughed also and said, 'I know that!' I had meant to ask him if he had watched a particular program on the TV the night before, but forgot. Shrugging, I thought I'd ask him next time I spoke with him (which was often). It became a big thing for me that I hadn't asked him, that we hadn't talked about this program that I knew he'd enjoyed. I knew in my mind that he had watched it because he'd rung me to tell *me* to watch it. But I was annoyed, felt cheated that we didn't get to talk about it. It's trivial, but it became so important to me.

Small things such as this become important. It's unfinished, no proper ending. Even if we did say goodbye, if the person we love is ill for many months or just a short time, there is always more we could say, more we want to convey. To just say *I love you* one more time.

Here are some attitudes to help make self-induced after-death communication easier.

1. Give yourself permission to enter into a new relationship with your loved one.
2. Be aware of your dreams. Write them down. When you go to sleep at night, ask for your loved one to visit you in your dreams. Give them permission. This is a great starting point.

3. There are many very great books on the subject of after-death communication. Read about these experiences. Exploring possibilities and raising your awareness is a step in the right direction. There is an excellent list of books at the back of this book.

4. Know that if your loved one does not communicate with you it does not mean they do not love you. As in the case with my dad, he simply did not know how. This may take some time for both of you.

5. Pay attention to how you feel. Sometimes feelings in your body may be an indication that you are being contacted. You may feel an overwhelming feeling of love. You may feel tingling sensations in your body. These are all ways in which we may experience contact.

6. Be aware of signs and signals. 'Funny stuff' does happen – don't dismiss it as trivial or coincidental! Coincidences, objects moving, odd noises, strange smells associated with your loved one (for example, cigarette smoke or a particular perfume) are all signs and signals that need to be observed.

7. Learn self-hypnosis. This is the fastest way I know to become more 'open'. Contacting someone who has died is like tuning into a radio station. First you must switch the radio on, then adjust the dial until you are on the right wavelength. Self-hypnosis allows you to switch on and tune in. I will include some guidelines to induce contact using self-hypnosis and visualisation at the end of this chapter.

8. When you do have contact, only discuss it with those special friends whom you know are accepting. Don't tell anyone who may put you down or trivialise your experience. Don't trivialise it yourself either. This is a precious gift indeed.

9. Make a firm decision to *adopt a belief* that there is no separation. Remember the wave/particle duality. In experiments the particle could behave either as a wave of energy or as a particle, depending on the *belief* of the person conducting the experiment. Your thoughts and beliefs do make a difference!

10. Be open. The saying goes, *The mind is like a parachute – it works better when it's open.*

So, if your loved one was trying to contact you, in what way do you think they would do this? As we have seen dreams provide a natural and fertile environment for after-death communication to take place. But also be aware of synchronicities, a feeling of a presence, smells and sounds of your loved one or objects being physically manipulated.

After my dad died, I had an area on top of my aquarium that just 'became' an informal altar – this was unintended, it just simply happened. There was a candle and a few photos together with his glasses and a few other bits and pieces. Oh yes, and his ashes.

It was about three months after my dad died, early one evening that I lit the candle along with others around the lounge room. It was almost time for bed and I remember looking over at the candle and being glad it had burned out because it was one less to snuff before retiring for the night. A moment or so later I looked again and the flame was burning as brightly as ever. I went over to the candle to have a closer look and, being aware that this might be my dad, I said a mental 'hello' in my mind. It went out again shortly afterwards.

Now, I have a 'thing' about leaving candles burning when unattended. I don't do it. I thought I would just go over and check one more time to ensure it had gone out properly this time. I did and it had. But knowing this was my dad, and knowing that the flame couldn't reignite because it was dead, I said to him jokingly, 'Alright, clever clogs (an affectionate name he used to call me when I was growing up), let's see you do it again,' and I walked away and sat down, satisfied that I had outsmarted him in some way. The first thing that happened, merely a second or so later, was a spluttering sound and I turned my head to see the flame spring to life as strong as ever. I jumped out of my seat in shock. My dad had most definitely contacted me, I had responded, saluted his message, and back had come the response. I have never ever seen a candle do this before in my life. I love candles. I light them regularly. But this one was very special.

It was sitting next to my dad's ashes. And it was his birthday – the first since his death.

These are sacred moments, a connection between souls. I think these experiences are normal, natural and happen to everybody. It's just that some people are more aware of them, more sensitive to them, whilst others may be oblivious.

Often, when our loved ones contact us, the message is very clear. We grasp it in an instant. When Dad visited me in my dream for the very last time, whilst I had some difficulty understanding what he was telling me at first (what he had experienced as he died), it was much clearer once he grasped my hand and I could feel his heartbeat. Once this happened I understood the message literally in a heartbeat. There was no doubt in my mind whatsoever. It was conveyed faster through tactile sensations than any words could convey.

Sometimes, however, it is more difficult to understand what is being conveyed. This may happen for a number of reasons. Firstly, our own grief can get in the way. If we are in the depths of despair then it is often difficult to grasp what is being communicated.

Sometimes our grief literally closes us down, makes it impossible for us to see, feel or tune into these experiences. However, dreams are often good at bypassing this issue as you are deeply relaxed and open to receiving. Hypnosis and meditation are also excellent for this reason.

Fear can also sometimes hinder contact. If this is a problem for you and you are fearful ask yourself this: *would my loved one want to hurt or frighten me?* Of course not! Often they just want to let you know they are okay, to give you a message of some sort, or to say goodbye.

Other issues relate to difficulty your loved one may have to grasp *how* to communicate with you in this new way, as in the case initially with my dad. However, don't worry if you don't get it first off, because in my experience they will just keep trying until you understand.

But sometimes we become our own worst enemy. Contemplate this: You and I meet for the very first time. You walk up to me, smile and in a very friendly tone of voice say, 'Hello', as if I were an old friend.

I look but hardly notice you. I turn and walk away without acknowledging your presence in any way.

Do you feel like communicating with me again? Would you pursue a conversation with me? Do you feel rejected?

What if I smile back and offer you my hand and return the 'hello' in similar tones? You are much more likely to engage in communication with me.

Whenever we discount 'something' as 'nothing' we are turning our backs.

Start to welcome these experiences. Look for them. Embrace them. Befriend them. Say 'hello'. Expect it to happen. Plan for it – you will still be shocked when it does happen, but plan for it anyway.

SELF TALK

Your 'self talk' is the manner in which you speak to yourself. If you are telling yourself that this won't happen for you, that you won't be able to communicate in any meaningful way with your loved one or that these things only happen to other people, then I would like you to do the following immediately:

1. Take out a clean sheet of paper and write, 'I can't communicate with my loved one because...' and fill in the blank. You might say something like, 'I can't communicate with my loved one because this would never work for me,' or 'I'm never any good at this sort of thing' and so forth. Whatever it is that you say to yourself, write it down.

2. Place it in a pan or heatproof bowl.

3. Take a match and burn it.

It's nonsense. This is for everybody. We can all do it. Replace that negative self talk with 'I can' and 'I will'.

Sixteen

RITUALS

It seemed to be a necessary ritual that he should prepare himself for sleep by meditating under the solemnity of the night sky...a mysterious transaction between the infinity of the soul and the infinity of the universe...

Victor Hugo

Creating sacred rituals can be an important part of re-kindling the link and staying connected with your loved one who has died. Rituals are an intrinsic part of our being, it's what we do naturally. All cultures perform them, without exception – especially surrounding death. Humans know, at the very deepest subconscious levels, that rituals create a bridge, a link with the soul of the person who has died.

When someone we love dies we lose our sense of connection and it is this that leaves us feeling bereft and lonely. If an illness has been protracted prior to death we may orient towards revisiting memories of this painful time or we may only be able to access memories surrounding the death itself. This all goes to keep us hooked into the feeling that we have 'lost' something, which in turn exacerbates our sense of loss. It may prevent us from accessing memories of some of the special moments in our relationship. This is counterproductive to after-death communication. Specific types of rituals allow us to link back in to the happy memories and thus engage with our loved one, to feel their sense of presence in our lives once again.

Rituals may be used as a way of communicating with your loved one. They provide another way of facilitating after-death communication, an opportunity to create the space and the mood where the two of you can talk.

Creating a special sacred ritual is one of the first steps to re-establishing and engaging in facilitated after-death communication. It provides a bridge, prepares the mind to engage.

Finding a ritual that is relevant to you and your loved one is important. Included here are some ideas to get you started and thinking along these lines. But it is important to find something that is relevant to you and your loved one.

Ask

The first ritual is so simple. Often it is the simplest things that produce the most profound results. Just ask in your mind. Ask your loved one to let you know they are okay. You might do this in the form of a prayer, but you can just as easily do it as you would if you were talking to them. This is actually quite a normal, natural thing to do.

Many years ago when Sam, our little Yorkshire terrier, died, I was devastated. He had had a stroke at the age of two and was crippled in one leg as a result. We had spent months nursing him back to health, and I think because of this we had a very close bond. One night after he had died I lay in bed and I thought *I wonder if I think about him strongly enough, if I could just see him.* I'd heard of people who could contact the dead and I wondered if I could also do it. Well, I pictured Sam in my mind, and thought 'come on Sam, let's see you'. In other words I was asking him to pay a visit.

Sam would lie in an unusual position when he was on me, his body snug against mine, with his head on my shoulder, in much the same way that you might burp a baby over your shoulder. Well, suddenly, I felt this weight on my body as I lay in bed and I felt his head on my shoulder. I was so shocked and scared, because I didn't expect anything to happen really. I sat bolt upright in bed, hit my sleeping husband several times and shouted, 'It's Sam, it's Sam, it's Sam,' as I whacked him. It was so real. I could feel him.

A friend and colleague of mine had a similar experience just by simply asking.

ANNETTE'S STORY

My Dad died when I was 24 and after some years, around the anniversary of his death, I really wanted just to see his face one more time. I was in bed between that waking and sleeping state and said, 'Please let me see his face', and there he was – very clear – just the face.

So asking just before you go to sleep at night, like Annette did in the story above, is an excellent time to do this as you quite naturally pass through hypnosis on your way to sleep. Alternatively, if you wake in the early hours of the morning this is also a good time to ask. Early morning seems to be the time when lucid dreams are more prevalent and you are most likely to have an after-death communication. The other time that can be of benefit is if you have a nap in the afternoon. Any time before you nod off to sleep is probably going to give the best results. This is a great step to take as it is so simple and often produces after-death communications that are closest to being spontaneous. Asking can be as simple as saying inside your head, *I just need to know you're okay*, or, *let me know you're okay*. Be patient. If at first you don't succeed, keep doing it.

MEMORY BOX

Creating a memory box is a beautiful idea. You can collect small but poignant things. Maybe a special piece of jewellery or a photo, an item of clothing or letters. Take your time thinking about what you would like to include in your memory box. At times when you want to talk with your loved one you can spend some time looking at and holding these special items. You may find at these times you feel especially close to your loved one. It is a way of connecting, building a bridge. Use these moments to talk to your loved one.

MAGIC WAND

When a loved one has died it is not unusual, even when we've had the chance to say our farewells, to wish that we could have done things differently, said something more. Maybe you didn't get this opportunity at all. Maybe the death was sudden, unexpected. Write a letter to your loved one telling them anything that you wish you had said or done differently before they died. This can be a very healing thing to do. They are going to get the message, loud and clear. Spend time preparing what you would like to say. This is your opportunity to say what you wished you could have said or done differently. Perhaps there is a poem you would like to include. Perhaps you might like to make up your own poem.

Ask yourself this question…

If I had a magic wand to wave and I could have done things differently, what would I have said or done to/for my loved one before they died? This will provide you with what you might like to say to your loved one in your after-death communication. Not that you need say it to them, they already know. But sometimes the 'saying' is for ourselves. It's healing.

You could keep this letter safe in your memory box. You can use this in your facilitated after-death communication a little later.

SPECIAL MEMORIES

Spend some time thinking about those very special memories. Find the most touching, poignant times and write about them. Include all those funny moments, perhaps where you've laughed the most. List all the special things your loved one has taught you. You may like to include these in your memory box also. This can be a powerful tool to use as a way of connecting with your loved one.

CANDLES

Lighting candles on special occasions such as on the anniversary of your loved one's death or birthdays and at other special times is a way of honouring and connecting with your loved one. You may like to extend this to lighting a candle before entering into a facilitated after-death communication with your loved one.

MUSIC

Music is a very evocative and powerful force. It transports us back in time in the blink of an eye. Playing your loved one's favourite piece of music will help you to reconnect and build that bridge.

PLANTING A TREE

Planting a tree or a special plant in your garden and perhaps placing a seat or a large rock to sit on nearby can give you a special place to 'be' with your loved one. A quiet place where you can pray or meditate or talk with your loved one.

These types of sacred activities help to bring about a sense of comfort and balance. All are about reconnecting and maintaining that connection with your loved one. You do not have to follow any of these. Find something that reflects the nature of your relationship.

It might be as simple as watching a sunset or going for a walk in the bush or along a beach in the early hours of the morning or in the evening. Talking with your loved one at these times can be a very real communication between the two of you. Whenever you do any kind of ritual in order to connect do not forget to listen. Be like the boy in the story, look with your soul and listen with your heart. Be aware of any signs that your loved one is communicating with you. They will certainly be aware of you communicating with them!

SACRED SPACE

Create a special place, a sacred sanctuary, in your home for reflection, meditation, prayer and communication. Make a small altar dedicated to your loved one. On the altar you might like to place candles, flowers, mementos, photos or anything that you feel is right.

Creating a dedicated place where you go when you want to talk with your loved one is like putting on a uniform to go to work, it shifts your attention and your energy and puts you in the mood. It's a way of letting yourself know what you are here to do. It creates the right energy and environment for communication. After a while, if you are sensitive, you may begin to notice that there is a very special energy created in this spot. It becomes a spiritual sanctuary for you and your loved one. This is indeed a special place.

If you don't have a dedicated room, just a small altar in your bedroom can be very beautiful. Alternatively, a small nook outside in your garden can make a perfect setting for sacred space, perhaps a place where you can watch a sunset or sunrise.

Take a few moments out of every day to simply be with your loved one in this space. This is your special place where you can go when you want to communicate with your loved one.

Seventeen

HYPNOSIS

What was it Adam had said about the 'You' magic? Oh yes, it was 'Close your eyes.' Jane closed them tightly.
And then he had said, 'Now think of another place, say where you were once happy.'
And then they were beside her, too, the man and the dog, and it was summer again...

The Man Who Was Magic

Paul Gallico

Hypnosis has been around for quite some time. This is not a modern invention. Just about all cultures worldwide have used some form of hypnotic or trance state to assist community members to heal themselves. Chanting, rhythmic drumming, music, dance or prayer is used in ritualistic ceremonies even to this day. From the voodoo ceremonies of Africa to the chanting in St Peter's Basilica to the didgeridoos of indigenous Australians, no civilisation is exempt.

In fact, archaeological findings in France show us that nomadic tribes made drawings on the walls of caves showing their hunting triumphs. These drawings appear to be positioned in such a way that as the sun sets in the hunting season it casts light on the drawings. This has led behaviourists to wonder if this could be to highlight the hunting scenes so they were the last thing that cave man saw before kipping down for the night. This could possibly be one of the earliest forms of creative visualisation and utilisation of positive suggestion.

Ancient Egyptians used sacred places known as Sleep Temples or Dream Temples over 4000 years ago. These healing sanctuaries were established to overcome a wide range of issues, including emotional, mental, physical and spiritual problems. This is much the way we still use hypnosis today.

Egyptians could be ensconced in a Sleep Temple for up to three days where priests and priestesses would facilitate a trance-like sleep (hypnosis), allowing them to go deep within themselves to find their own healing. Upon awakening the priest or priestess would interpret the person's dream to determine an appropriate avenue of therapy. I guess even back then they held an innate understanding that we each carry the seeds of our own healing deep within. Effectively the ancient Sleep Temple is the modern day hypnotherapist's office! I think the techniques are probably a lot slicker and quicker today.

You may remember in a previous chapter that we looked at brain wave patterns. Let's just revisit this for a moment.

Beta state occurs around 14-40 cycles or hertz per second and we call this waking state.

Alpha state happens at 7-14 cycles per second. When we are in Alpha state you may be daydreaming, relaxing or in a mild state of hypnosis. As you read this and are focusing on what you are reading you are probably relaxed and in a light trance.

Theta state is between 3.5 and 7 cycles per second. This is deep relaxation, deep hypnosis. Sleep and dreams also happen here.

Once brain wave patterns slow to Alpha, it is at these moments that spontaneous after- death communication is most likely to occur. The very act of slowing down brain frequencies which occurs in self-hypnosis will predispose a person to being receptive to these sorts of phenomena. There is a difference, of course, between spontaneous after-death communication and facilitated after-death communication. In spontaneous after-death communication, we are not actively seeking the experience – it's a surprise. Sometimes it's a shock. Conversely, in a facilitated after-death communication we are actively producing the right environment and stimulation for the brain in order to induce contact. However, it can still be a bit of a surprise, or shock, when it first happens. And it is no less powerful because of facilitation.

Hypnosis then is a normal natural phenomena that all people can, and do, access on a daily basis. In addition to experiencing hypnosis whilst reading a book or watching a movie, you also experience it each night when you go to sleep and also upon wakening in the morning. It is that dreamy in-between feeling you get.

Normally the subconscious mind is closely guarded by a filter system. This filter system allows some things in and blocks other things out. It is called the Reticular Activating System. It is semi-permeable and its job is to protect the subconscious mind. Hypnosis bypasses this system and allows a greater range of access to the subconscious regions of the mind. So in hypnosis we have greater access to long-term memory, emotions and to a large degree some unconscious bodily functions can be influenced.

It is when this filter system is relaxed, during a mundane task, such as driving a car or doing housework or during meditation or dreams, that relaxed time as you are drifting off to sleep, or just on waking, that we are most likely to experience a visitation from a loved one who has died. **Hypnosis is a direct way to access this state at will, making it perfect to facilitate after-death communication.**

So, it can be said that hypnosis is an altered state of consciousness. Consciousness is not static, but fluctuates constantly throughout the day and night. As we have already seen, many, if not all, instances of nearing-death awareness, after-death communication, out-of-body experience and also near-death experience occur when consciousness is in an altered state; consciousness is somewhere other than what we call the normal waking state known as Beta (14 to 40 cycles per second).

Accessing hypnosis is easy. You do it all the time. When you are engrossed in a book, as I hope you are right now, you are already in a light trance. When you are watching a movie, you are in a light trance. When you are focused on a task, you are in a light trance. When this happens peripheral awareness fades and we become more focused, less aware of other things that may be going on around us. When my husband sits down to watch the cricket, the house could collapse and as long as the TV remained intact, he probably wouldn't notice.

During hypnosis some people experience a light floaty feeling or a deep heavy feeling, like they are going to sink right through the chair. No two people will experience hypnosis in quite the same way, it's a unique experience for everyone. Whatever you experience is just fine.

The other thing you need to know is that there is no place that you will get to where you can definitely say, 'I've arrived, I'm in hypnosis now', because there are just lighter or deeper states of hypnosis. A lighter state is no better or worse than a deeper state. It simply just *is*. I have seen poignant after-death communications occur in just a light trance. So whatever level of trance you go to is probably just right for you. And of course, it is the nature of human beings to find things easier with practise, so each time you practise going into hypnosis you will probably find yourself going deeper and deeper and the images will become sharper and stronger. It's like a muscle, the more you use it the stronger it gets!

Again I stress to you a word of caution about using this method as a way of connecting if you are recently bereaved. It may be better to wait, give yourself time, before you engage in communication of this nature. But ultimately the decision is yours. You will know what is best for you. Be guided by your intuition.

LETTER OF LOVE

There are often so many things we would like to say to a loved one who has died, but when the moment comes we are speechless. Writing a letter of love will help you to define what you would like to say, how you would like to say it, what is important to say and what is not. It helps to bring order to your thoughts and feelings. When you begin to write, allow your words to flow from your heart. No-one else will read it, this is between you and your loved one only.

Here are some things to consider before you start. You do not have to write about all this, only the things that are most relevant for you and your loved one.

- When you were sick it was like...(if appropriate)
- When you died I thought...
- When you died I felt...
- Since you died I...
- I am angry because...
- In my body I feel...
- What I miss most is...
- What I most regret is...
- I wish I could...
- I wish we could have...
- I want you to know about...

- Life is different now because...

- If I could have done things differently I would...

- I love you...

- I will always...

- Thank you for...

- Anything else you feel is appropriate

This is hard. This may hurt. This may take you some time to complete. Take your time, there is no hurry. Let the tears flow as needed.

To begin, take a few moments to close your eyes and Breathe Peace, just bringing that feeling and colour of peace into your body. And when you are ready, take out some note paper and begin, as you would with any letter, Dear...

When you have finished it's time to nurture yourself again in some way, do something nice just for you. Go back to your journal and find that list of nice things to do for yourself. Pick one and do it.

Keep this letter of love for the next part of your journey.

Eighteen

LIGHT

And though he tried to look properly severe for his students,
Fletcher Seagull suddenly saw them all as they really were, just
for a moment, and he more than liked, he loved what he saw.
No limits, Jonathan? he thought, and he smiled.
His race to learn had begun...

Jonathan Livingston Seagull

Richard Bach

Well, here we are, and what a journey! I'd firstly like you to be aware that facilitated after-death communication may take on a life of its own, so to speak. Allow it to do so. These are very special moments that do not need to follow any set agenda. Also remember here that this is not a one shot wonder. You can repeat this any time you wish. Be persistent. If nothing happens the first time, remember it is the nature of human beings to find things easier with practice.

You may remember right back at the start of our journey I asked you to entertain the idea to *never let go*. Now into the cooking pot of your mind I'd like you to add a dollop of persistence, an attitude of *never give up*.

So if you are ready then let us begin.

THE RAINBOW

You might like to ask a trusted friend to read The Rainbow aloud to you, alternatively you can record your own voice. Ensure that there is a long pause between each passage to allow you the time to follow each instruction. Leave plenty time for communicating with your loved one also. Just take your time, there is no rush.

Firstly re-read your letter of love. There will be things in there that you might like to bring into this next journey. So just refresh your mind, though you probably won't need to. You will know what to say to your loved one.

Find a comfortable place to relax for a while, either sitting or lying down. You might like to loosen any tight clothing, take the phone off the hook, or whatever else you need to do to ensure that you are comfortable and undisturbed. This is your time, your opportunity.

Begin by clearly stating your intent, what you want to happen. This tunes your brain into what you want to achieve. It aligns your mind with your intention. It's a clear invitation to your subconscious mind and to your loved one.

Begin by taking a few nice deep breaths. Nice and easy....

And just imagine that there is a beam of pure light starting to form just below your feet. As it begins to crystallise and form just notice what colour this beautiful beam of light is. It can be any colour of your choosing....

This beam of iridescent light sparkles and shimmers and is filled with the radiant warmth of love and wholeness and trust. This light is infinite, it comes from nowhere and everywhere. This light weaves and spins a web between all things, connecting the past, the present and the future. This light is called the Light of Infinite Love.

Notice as this beam of light gently kisses the bottom of your feet, and as this happens you can begin to feel a warmth entering the very soles of your feet, bringing a deep feeling of tranquillity and peace and relaxation.

Just allow this healing light to wash gently upwards from your feet and into your calves, moving the warmth into the area of your lower legs. Notice how, as this happens, all the fibres in your legs begin to relax as the muscles soften and become like liquid.

Feel this light now pouring up into your thighs, softening, feeling the warmth, the relaxation, the peace, the healing that flows inextricably with this light.

As this light moves further up into your pelvis and your lower back and radiates outwards into your stomach, it softens the muscles of your abdomen and tummy, filling these places with radiant warmth, love and tranquillity and healing.

And gently, very gently, this light enters into the base of your spine, filling every space, entering every tissue in your spinal column, filling it also with this radiant light, love, peace and healing. Notice as your spine fills with this radiant warmth that is the Light of Infinite Love.

As it travels up the spinal column, notice as it radiates out now, inevitably spilling over into the nerves that exit the spinal column travelling to other parts of the body, the arms, the hands, the chest cavity, the heart... all filled with this beautiful, peaceful, iridescent light that is the Light of Infinite Love.

And as the light touches your heart, your heart begins to soften, gently healing any pain that might be held there. Sometimes when we have experienced intense emotional pain, the heart closes down, it hardens in order to protect itself from the river of sorrow that is our grieving. So just allow this light to linger here for a moment longer. And as this continues your heart begins to softly, gently loosen and soften around the edges, as it begins to open to the energy and healing properties of this light that is infinite. Fill your heart now, allow it to be flooded with this light, bathing it, enfolding it, filling it with healing bliss that is the song of this light. Notice that your heart begins to beat stronger, feel lighter, freer, more at peace, as the Light of Infinite Love begins to weave its magical web, a web of connection that spreads out from your heart way out into the universe, connecting you with all things from the smallest molecule that makes up your body, to the furthest most distant galaxy. Just know that all separation is an illusion. Feel the connection reaching out from your heart across the illusion of space and time.

Gently moving this incandescent light now further up the spinal column into the base of the brain, the little brain, the cerebellum. Allow it to gently enter into the cerebellum, that part of your brain that is at the top of your spine. Entering also into the limbic areas, the seat of your subconscious mind and finally spreading right throughout the cortical regions of your brain. Take a moment to notice, as this warmth spreads, bringing clarity of thought, it begins to heal any wounds that may be held here. When we have feelings of being overwhelmed with pain, engulfed in our grief, it is our mind that says to us, *I cannot cope, I cannot go on, why has this happened to me?*. We may feel these questions in every part of our being, but it originates here in the mind. Notice as this light of connection touches every part of your mind and brain, that it allows you to find new ways of talking to yourself, creative ways, gentle ways. As this light continues to move softly through and around your brain, it says to you 'hold on' 'nurture yourself', 'take good care of yourself'. Just open your mind now to this song that is the Light of Infinite Love.

From the depths of your mind and brain now let this light enter into your soul, your spirit. You do not need to know how to do this. Just imagine and it is so. When we grieve it is at the deepest levels of our soul that we are wounded most. It is our soul that aches for what is lost. Allow this light to bathe your soul now in its radiant infinite light. Notice as your soul re-energises, basking in this Light of Infinite Love. Feel the warmth trickling at first, then engulfing your soul in light.

Notice now how deeply relaxed you have become. Notice too, a rainbow of light as it begins to expand outwards from your heart, across time, across space, across the darkness that is grief, across the illusion we call life. This is the Rainbow of Connection. Notice the beautiful colours that make up this rainbow of light. And as this light radiates outwards it searches out, seeks and finally connects with your loved one. Again, you do not need to know how it does this. Just allow it to happen. As the Rainbow of Connection touches your loved one's heart you are both transported to a special place. It may be a special place that the two of you have shared at some point on your journey together, a beautiful garden somewhere or perhaps beside a lake or river. Just notice as you simply find yourselves there.

You embrace; it feels real because it is real. Just take a few moments to feel the warmth of this.

And it is here that you both find a comfortable place to sit. Maybe there are seats or maybe you just sit on the grass or the sand for a while. Whatever feels most comfortable. And this is your opportunity. Your loved one is waiting; they really want to hear from you. It may be that they want to speak first; if this is so, just allow it to happen. If you are harbouring any feelings of guilt then this is an opportunity to say what you need to say. If there is anything that needs to be forgiven then this is the moment. Perhaps it is neither of these things, but just some shared time together that you both need. Take your time. And let them respond.

Notice that your loved one has a special gift for you. It may be a kiss, or a hug, or a touch or symbol or something else entirely different. Accept the gift that is offered. You may have something you wish to give in return.

Ask your loved one, if you wish, to visit you in your sleep. Let them know how much you would like this...

It's time now for you to return. And you notice as you begin to journey back that this Rainbow of Connection remains, connecting your heart with theirs. The truth is there is no separation. Your loved one is here with you all the time. The rainbow serves not only as a reminder of this, but it is the very link, the bridge to your loved one.

You journey back into your body, and bring your awareness back into the room. Keeping your Rainbow of Connection, maintaining this connection that you now have, for as long as you need and always.

Just take a few moments to collect yourself and be present back inside your body and the room. Don't rush, there's plenty of time.

Take out your journal and record your experience. Do this in a sequential manner so it is easy to refer to and compare with future experiences whilst you journey in this way. Maybe nothing much happened if this is your first time; don't worry if this is the case. It gets easier with practice. Record your experience anyway.

You might like to consider the following whilst writing about your experience. Use it as a guide only.

1. Record what you saw. If you didn't 'see' anything, it doesn't matter. Other senses such as feelings and intuition are just as important, sometimes more so.

2. Write down what you heard. It's not uncommon on the first attempt at this that you might not hear your loved one speak. As previously outlined this can happen firstly because they may find it hard to communicate, secondly sometimes our own pain gets in the way of the communication and, thirdly, sometimes

we simply forget to listen. Listening is one of the hardest things we need to learn. Be patient when waiting for a response.

3. Now record what you felt. What feelings arose in you during your communication? You may have had a whole range of feelings or you may just have had a few. Did you feel feelings of love? Maybe you felt scared at first. Or sadness, or guilt. Whatever you felt write it down. If you were scared, ask yourself, *Would my loved one want to scare me?* Probably not.

4. Did you feel any physical sensations? Physical sensations can be just extraordinary and may often say more than any words. I am reminded of the hug my dad gave me during a dream visitation I had after his death. I had a pins and needles-like sensation right throughout my body. Similarly when he was trying to tell me about the heart attack he had and couldn't convey in words, he held my hand and I could feel his heartbeat. I knew in an instant. It was much more powerful than any words could convey.

5. What gift did they offer? Perhaps the gift was their presence, perhaps they gave you a symbol or sign. Perhaps it was a memory that flooded your being. Whatever it was write it down.

6. What else did you notice? Was anyone else present? As you think about this experience now, looking back, what do you feel? What do you think? What do you know?

Don't censure your writing, just let it flow. Be aware of any strange 'happenings' that occur after your self-hypnosis. Sometimes things just spontaneously happen directly after a communication of this nature; record anything that you feel is associated.

Doing self-hypnosis in this way during the evening can be an excellent way to allow it to spill over into your dreams and thus facilitate a spontaneous after-death communication. It is like you are offering an invitation to your loved one to visit. Record these experiences also in your journal. Remember you are beginning to form a new relationship with your loved one. Of course it will never be quite the same again. In many ways your relationship may now be more beautiful, spiritual and poignant than ever before. Allow it to continue to grow and flourish. Nurture it.

Death is an illusion. There is no death, only a return to reality. Reality as we know it to be - solid objects, matter, material objects - is all an illusion. Quantum physics tells us this. The true reality is that we are all one; there is no separation, no death. Surrender your old outdated concepts of death and know that all is one. Remember your wholeness. When our grief is at its most raw, we are in the depths of despair, we are focusing on what we have lost. Of course we will still grieve. This is normal. But our grief cannot be anything else but changed because of our connections. In reality there is no 'lost', your loved one is right here with you all the time. At the moment we call death, the soul transforms into reality. Sometimes, at very special moments in our lives, we get a peek at this reality. And it's beautiful, perfect. The spirit, soul or consciousness is merely transformed and you can journey into this reality at any time. Indeed, it belongs to you.

May your relationships forever flourish
and long may you continue to
Love After Death.
Blessings to you all...

EPILOGUE

If there ever comes a day when we can't be together
keep me in your heart,
I'll stay there forever...

Winnie The Pooh

A.A. Milne

SHADOWS

The boy woke up feeling stiff and confused. He looked around to remind himself of where he was. The ashes remaining from his camp fire were nearby, cold by now.

The boy slowly got up and memories of his dream came flooding back to him. *What amazing dreams I had last night,* he thought to himself. *First I dreamt that the old lady was here. And then the strange journey to my old village. I must have felt very lonely as I even dreamed of my parents.* And as he thought about his parents, for the first time he felt no sadness, only peace. *It felt so good talking to them, even if it was just a dream.* He remembered the conversation as if it had really happened; his mother telling him not to feel guilty for not having been there when tragedy struck. His father telling him how proud he was of the boy for having survived alone in the forest. And so many other things that cannot even be shared in thoughts, words that will remain engraved in his heart.

A pity it was only a dream, he thought as he got ready to start his journey. *But it felt so real and I feel better for it.* He picked up his wolf skin that kept him warm during the night and started folding it. *I have no proof that it really happened, but it does not matter.* And his thoughts drifted back to the man with no eyes, *some things do not need to be proved, only felt.* He was surprised at his own wisdom as he said this to himself. He had indeed learned many things since starting his journey.

He bent down to pick up his wooden bowl and noticed the strange mushy residue at the bottom. And in the back of his mind he could hear the old lady's voice asking him to drink from it. He shook his head and let the thought go. *It must be sand, blown by the wind during the night.* He rinsed the bowl in the stream nearby.

He packed his knife in the skin so as not to cut himself as he walked, and as he cast a last glance around the camp, he noticed the satchel on the ground. Confused, as he did not own a leather satchel, he bent to pick it up. It felt light, but there was something inside. He could tell by touching it.

The memory of the dream came rushing back. His mother holding his hands as they were about to part. Her soft eyes and her gentle voice. Her hand pressing a leather satchel into his hand and saying, 'I know that you do not need anything, because all you need is already within you. But take this, and if you ever feel like faltering on your journey, open it. It will give you comfort. If ever you feel alone, open it and we will be there with you.'

The boy stood in the morning sun, with the satchel in his hands, proof that it had not been a dream. But the boy needed no proof. What he felt in his heart was proof enough. It needed no explanation. He placed the unopened satchel away in the fold of his clothes and started walking east.

It was a pity that the boy was walking towards the sun, because he never noticed the two familiar shadows walking just behind him.

THE LAST STORY...

DAD

On the 8th of November, 2009, I make an unscheduled visit to Sydney's Mind Body Spirit Festival. My family and I are supposed to be heading up the coast for the weekend, but work commitments and weather conditions are unfavourable, and so we make a decision at the very last moment not to go.

Arriving with my daughter, Jessica, at the venue where the Mind Body Spirit festival is held each year, we make our way to the lecture room on the first floor. On this day Ezio De Angelis, a well known medium, is giving a Spirit Talk demonstration and I think it would be interesting to attend. This is a new experience for both my daughter and me, as neither of us have ever attended anything like this before. We arrive early and only a handful of people are scattered around the room that is to be packed, standing room only, within the next half hour.

Despite the fact that it is almost two years since my father has died, I am aware that this is a good opportunity to invite him into the lecture room with me. So as I walk towards the entrance of the lecture room I tell him, in my mind, 'Dad, this is a really good opportunity. It's now, mate. This is it. So just come in with me and wait there,' and I look to a spot just inside the door at the front of the room, where I want my dad to stand. 'Just wait there,' I tell him again, 'because this is a golden opportunity.' I am vaguely aware of his presence as he waits at the front of the room, just as I ask, and I wonder what will happen.

Jessica and I sit in the front row of seats, my dad just standing a couple of feet in front and to the left of where we are seated. Although I cannot see him, I know he is there.

Now, Muffin is a miniature Fox terrier, very tiny. I inherited her, along with my mum, when my dad died. She still lives with us, bringing the total number of dogs that we have to three. Meeting friends and casual acquaintances on walks with her is interesting – 'Oh, she's a Chihuahua, isn't she?' 'No, she's a Fox terrier,' I say. 'Oh, but she has Chihuahua in her, doesn't she?' 'No she's all Foxie.' And so the dialogue goes on. I admit, Muffin does look like a Chihuahua in the face, but she is all Foxie.

I'll be honest, the Chihuahua comments have become so commonplace that I have become a little dismissive in my tone of voice – there is a note of *I'm-not-entertaining-the-Chihuahua-concept-so-don't-keep-asking-me* kind of attitude.

Back to the lecture room. I am unsure what to expect. I am naturally quite sceptical; I know that there are many more frauds than the genuine thing. And so it is that we are there, Jessica and I, with my dad still standing at the front.

No one, not even the most sceptical person on this planet, could help but be deeply moved by what takes place in this room, on this rainy morning in November. We watch, eyes and ears glued, as one after another, Ezio proceeds to give very specific information to people about their loved ones who have died. It is as if he really is talking to the dead.

I lose track of time and I think maybe an hour or an hour and a half flies past at lightning speed. Drawing to a close, Ezio laughs and says, 'A little dog has just run into the room. It's a Chihuahua. It's run from over there,' pointing in the general direction of the door, 'and it's run to you.' He points with his fingers where the dog has come from and then directly to my feet. 'I think it's you.' Ezio is standing directly in front of me now, looking at me expectantly. 'It's run to you. It's a Chihuahua,' he insists. He walks over to where the dog came from, the very spot where I had asked my dad to wait, and says, 'There is a man standing here and he's put the dog down on the floor and said, "There you are," and it's run over to you. It's a Chihuahua. And it's sitting at your feet,' he insists as he stands directly in front of me.

My daughter nudges me and whispers, 'Go on, say something.' I whisper back to her my 'pat', no nonsense answer, 'It's not a Chihuahua.' I think mostly because I am in shock and partly because I cannot accept Chihuahua, I say nothing to Ezio. I just stare blankly at him. Because nobody could do that, could they? That's impossible. The medium moves on and closes.

I am so much in shock that the next day I ask my daughter if she also heard Ezio say, 'There is a man standing here and he's put the dog down on the floor and said, "There you are,"' because I just can't believe it. I think that perhaps I may have been hallucinating. I think time had just stood still for me at that moment and I had felt frozen.

My dad was there, just as I'd asked him to be. I knew beyond any shadow of doubt that he was there. Sending Muffin to my feet is significant because Muffin did indeed come to me; she lives with us and has become part of our family. She is also significant as she was curled up asleep on my dad when he died.

But this encounter was significant on yet another level, although I did not know it at the time. It was to be only three days later that I would ask my dad to 'wait there' once again, for an altogether different reason. And because of what had taken place, I knew without doubt that he was there.

3 DAYS LATER

MUM

*A*n old lady is assisted from her chair to her walking frame. She wants to go for a walk. She has been sick, but is recovering very well. She wants to go for a walk. She is frail but determined. She wants to go for a walk.

Her daughter holds onto her by the handles on the harness that is pulled firm around her thin body to give some support should she fall, whilst she holds onto the walking frame. They walk slowly down the corridor of the nursing home towards the dining room that leads out onto the patio, the garden a little further beyond.

They sit together, mother and daughter, marvelling at two cheeky little lorikeets that are hopping about from table to table and note the warmth of the sun and the lovely fresh air - such a beautiful spring day.

Within a few moments the old lady wants to go back inside. She is still breathless from the slow walk outside, but she has some dementia and forgets that she sat down only a moment ago.

On entering they realise that there is going to be a concert. The daughter asks her mother if she would like to stay for the concert. She nods and says she would. Knowing that her mum needs some oxygen fairly soon, the daughter encourages her mum slowly back to her room to get the much needed oxygen. It's hard to breathe.

Again she asks, do you want to go to the concert? Yes, I want to go. *So the daughter brings a wheelchair this time, knowing that the short trip will again steal the old lady's breath.*

At the front of the room a young and beautiful lady begins to sing. The song is unremembered, but the old lady knows it word for word. Something about turtledoves.

Knowing that her mum is happy singing away, a staff member is asked to keep a special eye out in case she gets short of breath. The daughter leans over and whispers to her mum that she must leave. She nods in response. The daughter again leans over and gently kisses her mum on the cheek and then places her own cheek in front of the old lady for a return kiss. The kiss is gentle and soft, like fairy dust. They exchange I love you's.

The daughter leaves. Remembering that there is some little thing that she has forgotten to do for her mum, the daughter walks briskly back towards her mum's room to complete the task.

Walking back down the corridor towards the concert room and eventual exit, the daughter thinks to herself, I'll just sneak quickly around this corner so she won't see me. *But lo, as she looks across to where her mother is sitting, the old lady turns her head sharply and looks directly into her daughter's eyes. The connection is instant. The daughter feels surprised, put off guard, like she has just been caught with both hands in the cookie jar. She smiles and waves. The old lady waves back. The moment is gone.*

Que Sera Sera, they sing. And the daughter hums on her way out of the nursing home.

This was to be the last time the daughter looks into her mother's eyes.

But this old lady has two daughters. And the next day there is to be a fete held at the nursing home. The elder of the two daughters pushes her mother in the wheel chair to look at the stalls. The old lady picks out a Christmas card that she likes the look of. Always loving bright and happy things, the daughter is surprised at her mother's choice. For instead of the pretty Christmas trees with baubles and tinsel or Santas or snowmen, the old lady has picked a card with a wreath on it. It is the only thing the old lady wants, and oblivious to the signs the daughter buys it for her mum.

The old lady slips silently from sleep into the oblivion of unconsciousness. Her breathing is laboured, but not unreasonably so. Her mouth open. Her face grey. Her daughters tend her. One of them, the youngest, bends down close to her mother's ear and whispers, Mum, in a while you'll see Dad, and when you do, go with him. He's waiting for you with a big wet sloppy kiss. Watch out for him and when you see him, just *go with him.*

Indeed, the man is waiting at the end of the bed, and the daughter, although she cannot see him, knows he is there.

Having some trivial (in hindsight) thing to take care of, the youngest leaves. She tells her mum she will be back very soon.

Sometime later the eldest must also leave. There is just an hour between one daughter leaving and the other returning. The eldest tells her mum that her sister will be back in just one hour. Just one hour.

The eldest leaves.

But an hour is not required, for soon after, the old lady sees the man watching her patiently at the end of the bed. He's waiting with a big wet sloppy kiss. She takes his hand, and they too leave.

It is a little over two weeks since my mother's passing and I have just this morning collected her ashes. They are sitting next to me on the table, neatly packaged, as I type. I am aware of her gentle presence. This book began with my dad, and it ends with my mum. I smile to myself because this is pretty much how it always was with them. Mum having the last word.

As I look at the finished product of this book, I realise it has indeed been one heck of a journey. Along the way I have stopped many times to look after my mum, who has been in and out of hospital twice, including a stint in intensive care with tubes in every orifice; to tend to my own health which has kept me firmly on my toes, and to...well, it's called living.

My dad's presence at the Mind Body Spirit festival, only three days before Mum died, brought comfort at a time when I would normally be frantic. As my sister and I had stood outside my mum's room on the day she was to depart, discussing what was happening, what the doctor had said and other pertinent issues, I felt as though in some way we were more part of a 'birthing' than a 'dying'. My dad's 'presence' made all the difference.

I feel like something has just been completed, but this has nothing whatsoever to do with the book. There are moments of sadness that are inevitable when someone we love dies. But the feeling of completeness is overwhelming. I feel at peace and the great need I had to keep my dad's ashes forever has just simply and magically vanished. They sit on top of my dresser in a ginger jar that I thought would always be there. But soon my mum's ashes will be placed there too. And at some point, in the not too distant future, at the right moment, in the right place, I will scatter them to the winds. Like their spirits, they too will be free.

DO YOU HAVE A STORY?

It would be a real privilege to hear your story.

If this book has touched you in some special way, or if you have had a special communication with a loved one who has died visit www.loveafterdeath.com.au and send me an email.

Warm wishes
Wendy

RECOMMENDED READING

There are many fantastic books on bereavement, grief and dying and all the wonderful associated phenomena surrounding death. Here are some of my favourites.

Bach, Richard, 1973, *Jonathan Livingston Seagull,* Pan Books, London. This cherished little book has graced my shelf for many years now, read and re-read many times over. Beautiful.

Bach, Richard, 1978, *Illusions – Adventures Of A Reluctant Messiah*, Pan Books, London. Just beautiful. Such wisdom.

Carroll, Lee, 2001, *The Journey Home - A Kryon Parable - The Story of Michael Thomas and the Seven Angels,* Hey House, Inc., California, Sydney. Mmm, I just don't want to tell you anything about this book, it is best left for you to discover. I think I have read it about a dozen times and each time it touches my heart.

Darling, David, 1999, *After Life – In Search of Cosmic Consciousness,* Fourth Estate Ltd, London. A fascinating read.

Dossey, Larry, M.D.,1989, *Recovering The Soul – A Scientific and Spiritual Search,* Bantam Books, USA & Canada. Although this book has been around for some time, it is a real treasure.

Edwards, John, 1999, *One Last Time,* Judy Piatkus (Publishers) Ltd. For those of you who have seen John Edwards working I know you need no comments here from me. He is just amazing. A very interesting and entertaining read.

Fenwick, Peter and Elizabeth, 2008, *The Art of Dying,* Continuum. A most excellent book, scientifically based. Another UK expert on near-death experiences.

Gallico, Paul, 1972, *The Man Who Was Magic,* The Hamlyn Publishing Group, London. I don't think this book is still in print, but you might find a second-hand copy through Amazon. I have had mine for years and I treasure it dearly. A wonderful little novel by a very wise man.

Kelley, Patricia and Callanan, Maggie, 1997, *Final Gifts : Understanding The Special Awareness, Needs And Communications Of The Dying,* Bantam Dell, New York.

Kübler-Ross, Elisabeth, 1976, *On Death and Dying,* Macmillan Company.

Kübler-Ross, Elisabeth and Kessler, David, 2005, *On Grief and Grieving – Finding The Meaning of Grief Through The Five Stages of Loss,* Simon & Schuster UK Ltd, London .

LaGrand, Louis E, 1999, *Messages and Miracles – Extraordinary Experiences of the Bereaved,* Llewellyn Publications, USA. This book is filled with beautiful stories of after-death communication. Very well written.

Levine, Stephen, 2005, *Unattended Sorrow*, Rodale Inc. Originally written as a pamphlet to that was to be distributed by the Red Cross to the bereaved of the September 11 disaster, he turned his writing into a book. It is beautifully written, compassionate, and is written in short, easy to digest chapters.

Parnia, Sam, M.D., Ph.D., 2006, *What Happens When We Die,* Hay House Inc. Carlsbad, USA. This really is a beautifully written book about near-death experiences. Sam Parnia is the leading expert on near death experiences in the UK.

Russell, Peter, 2005, *From Science To God – A Physicist's Journey into the Mystery of Consciousness,* New World Library, USA. For all your quantum questions, this is the book. It is simply written and easy to follow.

Sheldrake, Rupert, 2000, *Dogs That Know When Their Owners Are Coming Home And Other Unexplained Powers of Animals*, Arrow Books, UK. A very interesting read.

Van Praagh, James, 2000, *Healing Grief*, Hodder Headline Australia, Sydney. James Van Praagh is a very gifted medium and counsellor. This book is a must have for anyone interested in grief and the unusual experiences surrounding it.

Made in the USA
Middletown, DE
31 May 2018